# Daughter

## ACCEPTED - ADOPTED - BELOVED

## DR. LATATIA D. WHITAKER-RILEY

# DEDICATION

**To my parents...**

Mommy, thank you for valuing my life and CHOOSING to let me live. You have been the constant in my life through every trial and triumph. You have cheered me on. For all these things and so much more, I love you and dedicate this work to you.

Daddy, when you left me to go home to be with our Heavenly Father, it nearly took me out too. Nevertheless, I bless the Lord for your life and the impact you've had on my life. Many people could look at the life you lived and see only your struggles with addiction, but for me, you were and are so much more. You have always been my hero. A hero is someone who comes in and saves the day, and Daddy, you CHOSE to be that for me. Well Mr. Magoo, I love you dearly. Until we meet again, because you can't crown Him until I get there. Rest In Peace Daddy.

**To the love of my life...**

Mark, when you came back into my life you brought a breath of fresh air. You and I both talk about how we had all but given up on the idea of marriage. Oh, you will never know how grateful I am that God saw fit for us to find our way back to one another. Thank you for making me The Real Mrs. Riley. I love you beyond words, Riley.

**To my sons...**

First born, my whole life changed for the better because of you. When I held you for the first time, I was completely enamored, so much so that for the first two weeks of your life, I would not allow anyone else to hold or touch you. I was completely exhausted, and it was totally alright with me. Grandma Hattie (R.I.P.) had to make me go take a nap, lol.

You, son, are an anointed man of God. If the enemy would have had his way, you would never have made it into this world, but God... You are the epitome of "BUT GOD...". Because of some terrible choices I made prior to becoming pregnant with you, my body was threatening to abort you, but God... God has always had a plan and a purpose for your life. You matter on levels that you cannot even comprehend yet. Thank you for making me a better human.

Scooby...my baby boy. I know you are not my "baby" anymore, but you are now and forever will be a source of strength for me. God blessed me with a fiery, secretly compassionate force to be reckoned with. I know if nothing else, the bond we have as mother and son cannot be destroyed.

We have been through the fire, individually and together. One thing for certain and two things for sure, God has proven Himself yet again with us...We are more than conquerors through Christ Jesus. You too have been created by God on purpose, with purpose, and for purpose. The close encounters that you have had with death have both made the devil mad and proven that you are covered by the blood of Jesus Christ. Your fight makes me fight, and for that, I am forever grateful.

# FORWARD

*Daughter* is an AMAZING book! From start to finish, I was on the edge of my seat. Dr. LaTatia does a wonderful job laying down the foundation of her book, by explaining how the Orphan Spirit was first introduced into the world. She then goes on the explain the profound parallels between the concept of adoption in Christianity and the human experience of adoption, in her words, by telling her story.

Adoption reflects the love, grace and redemption offered by God. While reading Daughter, I was able to reflect on a few passages pertaining to the adoption spirit.

- Romans 8:5-17: This passage speaks about believers being adopted as children of God, receiving the Spirit of adoption, and becoming heirs with God.

- Ephesians 1:5-6: Here, Paul highlights how God predestined us for adoption to himself as sons through Jesus Christ, according to the purpose of his will, to the praise of his glorious grace.

- Galatians 4:4-7: This passage discusses how, when the fullness of time had come, God sent forth his Son, born of woman, born under the law, to redeem those who were under the law, so that we might receive adoption as sons. And because we are sons, God has sent the Spirit of his Son into our hearts, crying "Abba Father!"

- James 1:27: Although not directly about adoption, it talks about true religion being caring for orphans and widows in their distress, which can tie into the broader theme of adoption and caring for those in need.

In the journey of faith, we often find ourselves resonating with the profound themes woven throughout Scripture- themes of redemption, grace and belonging. Among these, few are as deeply resonant as the concept of adoption. As we embark on this exploration of the orphan and adoption spirit, we delve into a narrative that transcends earthly boundaries, echoing the very heart of God and His relentless pursuit of relationship with His children. In these pages, we are invited to contemplate the divine mystery of adoption. Both as a theological truth and tangible reality, reflecting the transformative power of love and grace in our lives.

I am extremely grateful to Dr. LaTatia for her unwavering dedication and insight in bringing forth this remarkable work. Through her diligent research and heartfelt reflections, she has illuminated the beauty and depth of the orphan and adoption spirit, inviting readers into a deeper understanding of God's boundless love and grace. May her words continue to inspire and uplift countless souls on their journey.

Gracefully,

Lady RaShonda K. Rhinehart

# PREFACE

The orphan spirit is something that many people struggle with, both in the Body of Christ, and in the world. As an adoptee, I personally carried feelings with me from the life I lived before I accepted Jesus Christ as my personal Savior, into my life as a born-again believer, feelings of rejection, worthlessness, fear, insecurity, inferiority, abandonment, and so much more. I did not know it then, but all those feelings, thoughts, and behaviors are attached to the orphan spirit. Who knew such a thing existed. I accepted God as Savior, but it was far more difficult to accept Him as Father, and much of that had to do with the trauma surrounding my strained and dysfunctional relationships with my earthly fathers, and yes, that is plural. What I began to learn and accept, however, is that the value that God the Father has placed on me is so great that He paid the price of my sins with the life of His only begotten Son, Jesus, the Christ, to restore me to His family (John 3:16). I am not a spiritual orphan, but a beloved daughter of The Most-High God through the Spirit of Adoption. (Romans 8:14-17)

It is by the leading of Holy Spirit that I am writing this book. It is an adaptation of my doctoral dissertation on *The Spirit of Adoption: Overcoming the Effects of the Orphan Spirit and, by Faith, Receiving God's Acceptance, Approval, and Unconditional Love as Sons and Daughters.* Through prayer, research and studying, the Lord revealed to me that this was not only written to partially fulfill the requirements of my degree; however, it is also meant to be the healing balm for many where wounds remain unhealed.

To understand the heart behind *Daughter: Accepted, Adopted, Beloved,* know that It is my intention for all who read this to understand through my research, adoption examples in the Bible, and my personal experience as an adoptee, that it is our heavenly Father's acceptance, approval and unconditional love that frees us from the bondage of sin, frees us to find our identity in Him, and to operate in our legal rights as heirs to the throne."

*Daughter* is meant to elevate the reader's understanding that the opposite of one who is abandoned, is one who is adopted. The various case studies all align despite the varying circumstances by which the abandonment and adoption manifested, in that the result remains the same; Adopted children, whether in the spirit or in the natural, are immediately endowed with the legal rights to employ the benefits of being sons and/or daughters of the adopting parent(s). In the life of the Believer, our adopting parent is God the Father, and that as His sons and daughters, we have rewards, rights, and responsibilities to govern our relationship with the Father and over our inheritance through our maturation into our identity in Him.

# Table of Contents

*Introduction* ........................................................................5

*The Orphan Spirit*............................................................ 13

What is The Orphan Spirit?...................................... 14

My Personal Experience with an Orphan Spirit ................... 15

*Biblical Examples of the Orphan Spirit*............................ 27

Ishmael................................................................27

Jephthah...............................................................29

Mephibosheth .........................................................30

The Prodigal Son .....................................................31

Gehazi.................................................................33

Uzzah..................................................................34

King Saul .............................................................37

Eli's Sons ............................................................37

*Orphanism* ...................................................................... 41

What is its origin? ..................................................42

*Fruit of the Orphan Spirit vs. the Fruit of the Holy Spirit* .. 45

Insecurity ............................................................45

Jealousy...............................................................47

Serves God to Earn His Love ...........................................49

Medicates Through Physical Stimulation .................................50

Driven by the Need for Success ........................................50

Uses People as Objects to Fulfill Their Goals..........................51

Repels Their Children..................................................51

Has an Issue with Anger and Fits of Rage ..............................51

Always in Competition with Others .....................................52

Lacks Self-Esteem.....................................................52

Materialistic.........................................................52

*The First Orphan*.............................................................. 55

Self-Will.............................................................56

Self-Exaltation.......................................................56

Self-Enthronement.....................................................57

Self-Deification ........................................................ 57

# Heart Condition .................................................. 61

# The Spirit of Adoption ...................................... 71
Justification ............................................................ 76

# Rights As a Daughter of God ............................ 83
Liberty in Christ ...................................................... 83
The Right to Choose ............................................... 85
The Right to Live .................................................... 98
The Right to Ask for What's Yours .......................... 105
The Right to Rule .................................................... 106
Exercise your Right ................................................. 108

# Privileges As a Daughter of God .................... 111
Intimacy in Relationship ........................................ 111
Abundant Life Here on Earth ................................ 112
Loving Discipline ................................................... 113
Authority & Power ................................................. 114
Security & Assurance Through Everlasting Life ....... 115

# Significance of Sonship .................................... 117

# INTRODUCTION

# Introduction

I am often taken back to a beautiful memory from my childhood. I was raised as my mother's only child for fifteen years. My bedroom was the place where I was free to dream, free to let my imagination run away. In my bedroom, I had twin beds with headboards that always reminded me of royalty. They were beautifully designed and girlie. My mother created a space for me that was the epitome of femininity. I would have royal tea parties with my dolls and stuffed animals. I would refer to myself as a princess while playing with them, but something happened one day. Those words pierced my soul, and I had an Epiphone. "I AM ROYALTY", I said to myself with a conviction and assurance that could have only come from the Lord. That moment never left me despite me not "living royal" all my life. It was not until years later, after I surrendered to Jesus Christ, that I understood that God always had a plan for my life, and that day, He allowed me to peek into my destiny.

All throughout the Old Testament, we see where God reveals His sovereignty over all creation. He introduces himself to Israel as "I AM", which encompasses everything about Him. They needed a home, and I AM created a nation for them and was the Ruler. He was also El Shaddai, the all-mighty and all-sufficient one who sustained them for many generations. The Israelites were surrounded by peoples and cultures that served and worshipped many different gods, which makes their revelation of I AM as the only living God most significant.

5

In Malachi 4:5-6, God declared: *"Behold, I will send you Elijah the prophet before the coming of the great and dreadful day of the LORD: And he shall turn the heart of the fathers to the children, and the heart of the children to their fathers less I come and smite the earth with a curse."* I AM left the people with this promise then went silent for four hundred years. Then in Matthew 3:17, at Jesus' baptism, God announced, *"This is my beloved Son, in whom I am well pleased."* This was the fulfillment of the promise in Malachi 4:5-6, and it was God's way of revealing Himself as *Father* to all humanity!

Even before He laid the foundations of the world, God's desire was to have a family and to be our Father. His goal was to be a father to those whose hearts would be knit to his. He desired it so much so that when it came to mankind, He did not just "speak" us into existence like He did with everything else. He took the time to orchestrate His design of all creation to ensure that when He came down to make His most prized creation, us, that all we needed to be sustained in this world would exist. According to Genesis 1:26-27, God said, "Let Us make man in Our image, according to Our likeness; Let them have dominion over the fish of the sea, over the birds of the air, and over the cattle, over all the earth and over every creeping thing that creeps on the earth." So, God created man in his own image; in the image of God, He created him; male and female He created them. Then, in Genesis 2:7, we read where the LORD God formed man of the dust of the ground and breathed into his nostrils the breath of life; and man became a living being.

This was the beginning of what was to be the most beautiful, intimate relationship between mankind and the Father. He provided a home, the Garden of Eden, and put man there. *"And out of the ground the Lord God made every tree grow that is pleasant to the sight and good for food. The tree of life was also in the midst of the garden, and the tree of the knowledge of good and evil. Then the Lord God took the man and put him in the garden of Eden to tend and keep it. And the Lord God commanded the man, saying, "Of every tree of the garden you may freely eat; but of the tree of the knowledge of good and evil you shall not eat, for in the day that you eat of it you shall surely die.""* (Genesis 2:8-9; 15-17). So that man would not be alone, God put him to sleep, took from him a rib, and made woman. Genesis 2:25 says that the man (Adam) and his wife (Eve) were both naked and unashamed.

Soon after, the serpent appeared in the garden and approached the woman (Eve). He cunningly manipulated the truth and tempted her. Eve was so enticed by what he said that she exaggerated God's command, believed the lie of the enemy, and encouraged her husband to join her in breaking covenant with God. They disobeyed His command to not eat of the tree of the knowledge of good and evil. It was at that moment that sin entered into the world and mankind was separated from the Father. Thus, the orphan spirit was unleashed into the world.

Since the fall of man, the orphan spirit has been at the root of much of the chaos, division, and destruction of the church and in the world. The spirit is rampant in the church and the world today. It is a mindset that

7

leads to a deadly heart condition that is rooted in that moment Adam and Eve were separated from union with God by their sin. There is an answer to this orphan spirit, which is the Spirit of Adoption and the Spirit of Sonship. Father God is waiting for his sons and daughters to understand who they are and to be the co-heirs He created them to be. Jesus is the perfect example of a son who knows his true identity, position, and inheritance.

Jesus left His Heavenly home to be born on the earth as a man, leaving His Father and His godly nature behind. As a child, He was raised for a time in Egypt, having escaped Herod's mass execution in His earthly home. As he began His ministry, He was continually on the move with His disciples going from town to town and being unwelcome in many places. He had no earthly home, yet He never felt the sting and pain of the orphan spirit because he was constantly with His Father. The gospel of John gives us this quote from Jesus about sonship: *"When I am raised to life again, you'll know that I am in the Father, and you are in Me, and I am in you."* (John 14:20).

Jesus said in John 3:13, *"No one has ascended to heaven, but He who came down from heaven, that is, the Son of man who is in heaven."* Jesus, of all men, did not have an orphan spirit. He was at home wherever He happened to be physically, because He and His Father never lost the connection... not until He took our sins upon the cross. There He partook of the orphan spirit when He cried out in anguish, *"Father, why have you forsaken me?"* Only then did Jesus experience the pain of the orphan spirit, as He died to bring us back to a relationship with our Heavenly Father. Now, we can come back to the Eden that the Father created for us, and we can live *from* Heaven, instead of *toward* Heaven.

From the details of my personal experience and a deep dive into the Scripture, clarity of God's Spirit of Adoption and the answers to many other questions will be realized over these next pages. We will unpack my adoption story, and it is my hope that after perusing the following pages, readers will have their faith deepened, and hearts healed.

# Part 1:
# The Orphan Spirit

# Chapter I

# The Orphan Spirit

Sonship in the kingdom of God is a term used for both genders to refer to those that the Spirit of God has adopted. The orphan spirit is perhaps the greatest curse on the earth today. Ever since Adam and Eve were alienated from God the Father in the Garden of Eden, an orphan spirit has permeated the earth, causing untold damage. Only when a person is healed of fatherlessness through the love of God is the orphan spirit broken so they can begin the process of entering mature sonship. Sonship is so important that all creation is presently crying out for the manifestation of the mature sons of God. (Romans 8:19)

## What is The Orphan Spirit?

Feeling like an orphan can be debilitating. By "orphan", I am referring to a sense of abandonment, loneliness, alienation, and isolation. It has to do with perceiving in your heart that you have no real heritage, no sense of security in feeling protected, no inheritance, and no one really cares about your destiny. Most people affected with the orphan spirit also feel and fear abandonment. Almost immediately after the fall in Eden, the fruit of this orphan spirit resulted in jealousy, ultimately causing Cain to murder his brother Abel because God the Father did not receive Cain's offering. (Genesis 4) To make matters worse, in modern society, with the breakup of the nuclear family, large numbers of people are not only alienated from God but are brought up without the loving care and security of their biological fathers.

The orphan spirit is a demonic spirit that invades a person's mind causing them a sense of abandonment because of past hurts and experiences. It attacks the mind and emotions of the individual suffering with abandonment, rejection, and great disappointment.

An orphan spirit attaches to a person who has experienced extreme rejection in their life. It creates separation, worry, anxiety, anger, and fear. Once this spirit enters into a person it becomes a stronghold in their mind and remains there until a new foundational truth of the Word of God is formed. If this mental fortress is not corrected and torn down by the individual who accepts it, it will continue to the next generation until someone stands in the gap and says no more.

# My Personal Experience with an Orphan Spirit

Jackie (my mom) and Ronnie (my dad) were just kids when they met and Ronnie fell head over heels in love with her, but they were young, so being totally committed to one another had proven to be quite the challenge. Now, while they dated primarily exclusively, there were times that they did not see eye to eye and spent time away from one another. It was in those times that they dated other people, and for my mom, Foxx just so happened to be around. She and Foxx dated, became intimate, and that resulted my mother becoming pregnant with me. This is where I am told things went really off course. You see, my mom told Foxx about the pregnancy and the response she got in return was all but devastating. Apparently, Foxx was not interested in being a father to the child that my mom was carrying, and now, no longer interested in any kind of relationship with my mom. In fact, I am told that when she told him she was pregnant, he in turn responded telling her that she could "live and hope" if she thought he was going to be there.

Now, an unwed, pregnant teenager, my mom was faced with stepping into adulthood and parenting all at once and all alone, or so she thought. You see, although she and my dad were on one of their break-ups, his love for her was never ending, as was hers for him. She told me that when he heard the news of her pregnancy, yes, it was hard for him to accept at first, however, he made a choice that not many men would make. He chose her and he chose me. Charles Ronald Anthony Whitaker chose to be the father to my mother's unborn child, another man's unwanted, rejected,

15

abandoned child...little old me. When I was born, my daddy (Ronnie) was there, and he signed his name on the dotted line as father of the child. From that day until March 30, 2017, when he drew his last breath on this side of heaven, he gave every effort to being the best dad he was capable of being to me. Undeniably, he had his own life's struggles along the way, which left some holes in my life, but for as much as he had the capacity to love, he loved me.

One of the things that I looked forward to most as a kid was spending time at my grandmother's house. It was always a good time to be had when the cousins, aunties and uncles came together. Laughter was imminent. Grandma, Mommy, and my aunties would get together and make the most incredible meals while all of us children would run around, playing, and enjoying one another. Because I was the oldest grandchild, I often got to spend time with the young adults in the family and hear some things that I probably should not have heard.

One day in particular, a few of my older cousins (second cousins) and I were sitting on my grandmother's front porch laughing and joking, telling stories, and joning on one another when this man that I remembered only seeing a few times before, drove up in front of the house. Every time I saw him, he was quite cordial, greeted everyone, and always wanted to talk to my mom and grandmother. One of my uncles never seemed to be fond of the man, but everyone else was nice to him and appeared happy to see him when he came around. I had not had any personal interactions with him that I can recall at that point, but he would always smile, nod and wave when he saw me. Being the generally happy go lucky kid that I was, I would wave back and smile. This day proved to be much of the same except this time one of my older cousins turned to me and said, "You know who that is don't you?" "No, who is it?", I said. "That's your real father.", she told me. I was thoroughly confused. My ten-year-old brain could not comprehend what she was trying to say to me. She must have seen the confused look on my face and further explained, "Ronnie is not your real father, Foxx is.", referring to that man with whom my mom is now in deep conversation. What a random, jaw-dropping announcement coming from a twentyish-year-old to a ten-year-old. Judging by the painfully awkward silence that suddenly seemed louder than anything else, the rest of the family seemed to be shocked that she told me that as well, but not shocked at its truth. Breaking the silence with laughter, I began to argue that she was making stuff up, especially since we were all just joning on one another, but she stood firm and never backed down. Years went by before I ever spoke of that day again, however, I rehearsed it time and time again in my head.

In fact, a year or so after she dropped that information on me, Foxx appeared again. The family was gathered again at Grandma's on that summer's day. The adults were sitting on the porch while I and the rest of the kids ran up and down the street playing with the other children in the neighborhood. Out of nowhere it seems, this beautiful shiny black Cadillac Deville pulls slowly in front of my grandmother's house. Once parked, out steps this tall, fairly attractive man with what my grandmother would describe as a "sheepish" grin on

17

his face. What I took note of this time that I had not really paid any attention to before was that he would never come inside the gate. My mom walked over to him, and they had a private conversation.  Just then, the ice cream truck pulled up playing the happiest songs, attracting the neighborhood kids.  I remember asking mommy if I could have some money to buy something when she gave him this intense look.  That was the day he bought me a 25-cent popsicle and puffed his chest out with pride.

Shortly thereafter, my mom and I got into the car with this man, and we took a ride in his beautiful car.  He took great pride in that car instructing us to clap our feet so that we did not bring in any dirt, and we had to wait until I finished my popsicle.  He drove through the city very slowly as to avoid any bumps or potholes.  We finally got to our destination.  It was a Pic-n-Pay shoe store.  My mom and I went in, and I tried on a few different pairs of shoes.  When we finally decided on a pair, Foxx paid ten dollars plus tax, and again puffed his chest out.  He then took us back to my grandmother's and left.  I did not see or hear from him again for several years.

Now, in my sophomore year of high school, for whatever reason all of the aforementioned events began to flood my mind even more than before.  So many things had changed in my life from that last encounter with Foxx, the man who was said to be my biological father.  You see, Ronnie, the man I had come to know as daddy was finally back home with us, he and mommy had another baby, and we were once again a happy family; yet there was this lingering question…Which one of these men is really my dad?  So,

I asked my mom, all the while, remembering the thoughts of me being royalty.

The way I remember the story being told to me by my mother was that my parents separated when I was around two years old. When that happened, my dad went to live with another woman who had children of her own, three of whom were minors around my age and lived with them. Albeit my parents did the best they could to co-parent and trade weekend visitation, their separation left my mom to raise me for the next twelve and a half years primarily alone (My Grandma and Aunties helped a lot). While that may have been the case, I so treasured the time my dad and I shared together.

In hindsight, I was quite resentful that he did not live with us for most of my youth and that those other children got the benefit of having him there all the time. Perhaps, that is why I cherished the times that we did spend together so much. Although he lived with another woman and spent most of his time with her children, daddy made sure our time was special, and I was made to feel like his princess, the most important person in his life whenever we were together. That caused a bit of a rift between me and the other kids, as I was allowed access by my father to people, places, and things that they were not granted access to. I also was not subject to the same punishments as they were when I would get into trouble because my father's grace towards me was abounding. Daddy was to me the earthly representation of our Heavenly Father.

Something was happening in my life that I did not come to realize until I began to mature in my Christian walk and started evaluating some of the choices I had made and the pain it caused me and others. I had what the world likes to call "Daddy Issues". I was still carrying anger and resentment towards Foxx and trying to overcompensate his for rejection.

As a pre-teen, my behavior really began to take a turn for the worse, and the older I got, the worse off my behavior was. What I know now is that I was searching for identity, purpose, understanding, belonging, significance, security, and love. Stay with me and I will elaborate more throughout.

My family has encountered this spirit repeatedly throughout generations; however, the enemy has been defeated. When I was twenty-one years old, my first husband and I separated. I had recently come home from the Army. He was still enlisted in the Marines and stationed at Camp Lejeune, and I was living here in Maryland. It was our second pregnancy, and unfortunately, we miscarried. About a week or so after miscarrying our child at home alone in the bathroom, I was admitted to the hospital because I had become sick and needed to have a DNC (dilation and curettage) procedure. While I was in the hospital, my then husband had come up from North Carolina on special leave to be with me. Before coming to pick me up from the hospital, he stopped at our apartment. To date, I still do not recall what he said he stopped there to look for, but he had come across some pictures of mine taken before we were married during my time at Fort Ord in California. They were pictures of me and a male friend.    Although when he and I enlisted into different branches of service we agreed that we would keep in touch but date other people. Actually seeing me with someone else did not set well with him.

Now, he waited until we were home from the hospital to ask me about the pictures, I answered him honestly. He then thought it was a good time to tell me that he had been sleeping with a girl who hated me since junior high school, and that while he and I were planning our wedding, she had given him a son. Everything he said after that sounded like Charlie Brown's teacher to me. When it was finally my turn to speak, I put him out of the house.

My emotional response to this act of betrayal was to not care about anyone or anything because apparently, no one cared about me. After the initial shock and what I would have considered to be a brief time of grieving, I became like a wild animal...clubbing, drinking, sleeping around. I honestly could not tell you if I was using all of that to numb the pain, or if I was actually trying to prove to myself that if I tried hard enough, someone, anyone, would pay enough attention to me to want to love me the way I felt I should be loved. And then I met him...the father of my oldest living child.

He was a DJ at a club I frequented.    When I clubbed, everyone knew I was there. I made sure of that. You see, I danced from the time I walked in the door until the lights came up, and I danced hard. So, he learned my name, began to give me "shout outs" over the mic, would send me drinks, and then I started getting into that club and any club he was working for free, except it really was not free. We started meeting for breakfast after the club, getting to know each other. And then we started sleeping together. My divorce was not yet final, but back then, I did not care. At that time, I was so broken that I could not care less about anything other than what pleased me, and what pleased me was that some man was paying attention to me. Little did I know he was "paying attention" to a several other women also.

It started out being a lot of fun with the DJ, and in the beginning, we were spending a lot of time with each other, and talking a lot, then it started to fade. Things were changing and I started asking questions. The answers were not what I wanted to hear, so I broke it off with him. I began to think I should take some time for myself, and I did. But was it too little too late? Shortly after the breakup, I found out I was pregnant again. What a complicated time that was for me. You see, I did not want to tell him because I did not want him to think it was some low-down plot against him, and I really wanted nothing more to do with him anyway. My best girlfriend at the time was dating the DJ's cousin and she spilled the beans. So, guess who came knocking at my door pretending to want to be a father?

Cutting to the chase, I gave birth to my oldest son at Columbia Hospital for Women, surrounded by my mom, aunt, and grandmother. Mr. DJ was nowhere to be found. My son and I were in the hospital for four days. Mr. DJ did manage to make his way there to visit and hold him on day 3. A few weeks after we were released, he came by to visit empty-handed, and attempting to sleep with me. NOT!!! Despite the attempts that I made to have him spend time with his son (not with me), the very next time they would lay eyes on one another was in the court room at the child support hearing. As I think about it now, he was something of a Nick Cannon with babies everywhere. My son and two other children were born just weeks apart, and he was proud to claim them all. The difference between him and Nick though was that Nick could financially afford to take care of his.

Now, fortunately or unfortunately, depending on how one might look at it because I had not yet been saved, healed and delivered from the orphan spirit, my son was about to experience the effects of my choices and have an "orphan spirt experience" very similar to what I had experienced.

After finally getting divorced, I met a man who not only took a liking to me, but immediately, without being asked to, made a conscious decision to "father" my now two-month-old son. We met at a party and became instantly connected. Soon thereafter, we started dating, like mature adults should date. He came by to pick me up for our date and not only had a gift for me, but he had a gift, diapers, and milk for my son. That was over twenty-eight years ago, and he is still fathering him. After being together close to a year and a half, we had son together and married a couple of years after that. We were together ten years before we separated because of infidelity from both sides. Although he and I did not make it as husband and wife, he has been an amazing father to the boys. My oldest son had no clue that he was not his biological father.

After our breakup, I dated and married yet again. He had four children to my two. Those were the most miserable seven years of my life. He and his children were physically and mentally abusive to both my children and me, and he was even spiritually abusive. It was the conversations with him that brought me to the moment of telling my eleven-year-old son the truth about who his father really was. My third husband was so mean-spirited that he had threatened to tell my son if I did not. Well, not surprisingly, son was devastated, and reacted in a very similar manner as I did when I found out about my dad; he became withdrawn. He shared with me years later that he had so many questions in that moment, but his young mind really could not process it all. I knew that feeling all too well.

*"The Lord is near to the broken hearted and saves the crushed in spirit."*

*Psalm 34:18*

# Chapter II

# Biblical Examples of the Orphan Spirit

## *Ishmael*

God promised Abraham that he would be the father of many nations and that he would have a son. Through this revelation, God introduced himself at the progenitor and sustainer of Fatherhood. However, in Genesis chapter sixteen Sarah suggests that Abraham should have a child with her slave Hagar, an Egyptian. Now, it seems that this was a common practice at the time, as we see it also practiced in Genesis chapter thirty by Jacob's wives. The wife would give a female slave to her husband, but any children born would be counted as the children of the wife, perhaps an ancient version of surrogacy. While this may have seemed like a workable solution for Abraham and Sarah, in actuality it caused more problems than it solved.

Hagar did conceive a child with Abraham. When Hagar knew she was pregnant, she began to "despise" Sarah, and Sarah went to Abraham for help. Abraham told Sarah to do as she saw fit, so she began to mistreat Hagar, and Hagar ran away (Genesis chapter sixteen, verses four through six).

The angel of the Lord found Hagar in the desert and told her to go back to Sarah. He then told her about her yet unborn son: *"You are now pregnant, and you will give birth to a son. You shall name him Ishmael, for the Lord, has heard of your misery. [Ishmael means "God hears."] He will be a wild donkey of a man; his hand will be against everyone and everyone's hand against him, and he will live in hostility toward all his brothers"* (Genesis chapter sixteen, verses eleven and twelve). So, Hagar went back and gave birth to a son; Abraham was eighty-six years old.

In Genesis chapter twenty-one, Sarah's son, Isaac, is born, and once again problems arise. Sarah sees Ishmael mocking the young Isaac, and she demands action from Abraham: *"Get rid of that slave woman and her son, for that woman's son will never share in the inheritance with my son Isaac"* (verse ten). The matter distressed Abraham greatly because it concerned his son. But God said to him, *'Do not be so distressed about the boy and your slave woman. Listen to whatever Sarah tells you because it is through Isaac that your offspring will be reckoned. I will make the son of the slave into a nation also because he is your offspring'"* (Genesis chapter twenty-one, verses eleven through thirteen). *Abraham gathered some provisions and sent Hagar and Ishmael away. After the provisions had been exhausted,*

Hagar and Ishmael were overcome with grief, assuming that they would die in the desert. God heard the boy crying, and the angel of God called to Hagar from heaven and said to her, 'What is the matter, Hagar? Do not be afraid; God has heard the boy crying as he lies there. Lift the boy up and take him by the hand, for I will make him into a great nation.' Then God opened her eyes and she saw a well of water. (In the desert) So she went and filled the skin with water and gave the boy a drink" (verses seventeen through nineteen).

Once again, God appeared to Hagar and promised that Ishmael will be a great nation. Finally, we are told that, "God was with the boy as he grew up. He lived in the desert and became an archer." While he was living in the Desert of Paran, his mother got a wife for him from Egypt (verses twenty and twenty-one).

## Jephthah

Jephthah was the illegitimate son of Gilead and a prostitute. "...His half-brothers said to him, 'You shall not have an inheritance in our father's house, for you are the son of another woman'." (Judges, Chapter eleven, Verse two). The orphan spirit entered him in that moment. He was disinherited, rejected, and wounded in the house of his father. Jephthah fled, and the Lord brought to him, like He did for David, an army. Then Ammon invaded Israel and the elders came to him, begging for help. They invited him back and accepted him as leader.

Now, Jephthah could have said, "But you drove me out, you hated me," but he rose above that orphan voice. He defeated the Ammonites, and Ephraimites, forty-two thousand of them, and became judge over Israel for six years. No wonder Hebrews chapter eleven, verse twelve says he was a man who "conquered kingdoms, performed acts of righteousness, obtained promises". He overcame the orphan spirit and embraced his destiny.

## Mephibosheth

The Philistine army attached Israel at Gilboa and overcame them. Jonathan and his father, Saul, were viciously killed in battle. As the news reached Israel, the royal staff scrambled out of fear. In the midst of all the confusion, tragedy struck. Jonathan, son of Saul, had a son who was lame in both feet. He was five years old when the news about Saul and Jonathan came from Jezreel. His nurse picked him up and fled, but as she was hurrying to leave, she dropped him, he fell and became crippled. His name was Mephibosheth. (Second Samuel chapter four, verse four)

Mephibosheth not only had to battle with crippling limitations, but he also had to contend with being orphaned and alone. In many ways, his life was filled with disappointment and disaster. I believe that many of us can identify with Mephibosheth. Where there was once tremendous promise, only disaster remained. One from a prestigious royal line had been forgotten. Now, you do not have to be physically maimed or fatherless to be overcome with feelings like this. In many ways, what I am talking about is the impact of the "orphan spirit."

Years later, the subsequent king—David—wanted to determine whether there were survivors from Saul's household that he might honor. *"The king asked, 'Is there no one still left of the house of Saul to whom I can show God's kindness?' Ziba answered the king, "There is still a* son of Jonathan; he is crippled in both feet." (Second Samuel Chapter nine, verses three and four) Mephibosheth was located and escorted back to the palace. In the ancient world, it was common to destroy the entire bloodline of foes. So, Mephibosheth was legitimately concerned about standing before the king but, David was motivated by Godly honor and love. He did not want Mephibosheth harmed. He wanted him restored. *"Don't be afraid,"* David said to him, *"for I will surely show you kindness for the sake of your father, Jonathan. I will restore to you all the land that belonged to your grandfather Saul, and you will always eat at my table"*. (Second Samuel, Chapter nine, Verse seven)

Mephibosheth genuinely did not know what to do with the king's abundant generosity. *He bowed down and said, "What is your servant, that you should notice a dead dog like me?"* (Second Samuel, Chapter nine, Verse eight).

When Mephibosheth says, "I'm a dog", it confirms self-perceptions. He sincerely believed that he was merely a castoff of a fallen line. Against the backdrop of the king's goodness and grace, Mephibosheth's distorted identity becomes evident.

### *The Prodigal Son*

In the fifteenth chapter of Luke, is this parable of two brothers and their father, and the younger of the two sons demands that his father give him what he thought he was due, then he left home to live a very reckless life. After spending all that his father had given him, he found himself penniless, hungry, and destitute, so much so that he ended up sleeping with pigs. In the fifteenth chapter of Luke, verses seventeen through twenty, the bible says that after all of this, the young man "came to himself" and went back home to his father, to whom he later confessed that he had sinned. The father had compassion on him and received him as his son with open arms.

Many people overlook the behavior of the older son in this parable. While he was a bit more responsible in that he did not go off into the world and squander his inheritance, he was struggling with the orphan spirit himself. When the younger brother returned home, the older brother's jealousy was exposed. His obedience to his father was grim duty, not loving service. In verse 28, he was angry while his father was happy. He did not care that a great weight had been lifted from his father's heart. He thought only of himself and looked on the whole scene with jealous eyes and bitterness in his heart. Notice in verse 12 that the elder brother received his inheritance when his younger brother received his. In fact, under Jewish law, the eldest son received a double portion. He had nothing to lose by his brother's return, and yet he was bitter.

Like many people, the older brother could not see anything wrong with his behavior or mindset. He could only find fault in his brother and father. In verse 29, he tells his father that he had never disobeyed one of his commands. And the Pharisees thought the same thing about God. There was even one group of Pharisees who actually kept track of all that they did for God so they would know exactly how much God owed them. he older son was also self-centered, filled with self-pity, loveless, and ungrateful.

So, in this chapter of Luke, we have not one, but two prodigal sons. One left for the far country while one stayed at home. One became an alien through sins of the flesh while the other became an alien through sins of spirit. One found himself eating the rinds of worldliness while the other ate the rancid food of a sour and angry mind. One shows us what outward sins do to our lives, while the other shows us what inward sins do to our hearts.

## *Gehazi*

In II Kings 5, the Bible records the story of Gehazi, the servant of Prophet Elisha. When we compare the life of Elisha as a servant of Elijah and the life of Gehazi as a servant of Elisha, we see a sharp contrast. Whereas Elisha served Elijah faithfully to the end and received a double portion of the spirit of Elijah, Gehazi, because of his unfaithfulness, only received the leprosy that Naaman had been afflicted with. Elisha was described as one who poured water on the hands of Elijah (II Kings, 3:11B). In other words, he was Elijah's servant.

Gehazi was a greedy servant of Elisha. It is believed that the day he was caught, was not only the day he took something that was not meant for him, but he had been doing it until his cup was full. He was caught and cursed.

Greed can be said to be an unreasonable, insatiable longing for material gain, food, money, status, power, etc. When a person is greedy, it means that they cannot be satisfied or contented with what they have.

33

This will lead to devious acts. A greedy man cannot be satisfied with what God has given him, and he cannot be satisfied even with God because he will always go extra mile to get what he wants no matter what. Greed is a killer, and it corrupts. It makes a person not to be spiritually connected.

## *Uzzah*

I Chronicles, 13:1-3 (Also told in II Samuel, 6) introduces an incident containing a presumptuous act, immediately followed by a sobering display of divine justice. However, this time, one of the most respected names in Israelite history is directly involved. It is the story of Uzzah's sudden death while moving the Ark of the Covenant, the most sacred and revered of Israelite objects. The Ark, representing the throne of God and containing the tablets of stone that Moses received from God on Mount Sinai, normally resided in the Holy of Holies.

David desired to move the Ark to Jerusalem to continue to consolidate the kingdom under himself. As they were moving it on an oxcart, the oxen stumbled, and the Ark appeared to be toppling to the ground. Uzza, in what may have been pure reflex, put out his hand to steady the Ark, but upon touching it, he was immediately struck dead (verses nine and ten). At first, David was angry that God ruined his party (verses eight and eleven) - as the whole atmosphere of the Ark's transfer was celebratory - but shortly after, he became extremely fearful (verse twelve).

God had given strict instructions for transporting the Ark, found in Numbers 4:4, 15, 17-20:

> *"This is the service of the sons of Kohath in the tabernacle of meeting, relating to the most holy things: . . . And when Aaron and his sons have finished covering the sanctuary and all the furnishings of the sanctuary, when the camp is set to go, then the sons of Kohath shall come to carry them; but they shall not touch any holy thing, lest they die. These are the things in the tabernacle of meeting which the sons of Kohath are to carry. . . Then the LORD spoke to Moses and Aaron, saying: "Do not cut off the tribe of the families of the Kohathites from among the Levites; but do this in regard to them, that they may live and not die when they approach the most holy things; Aaron and his sons shall go in and appoint each of them to his service and his task. But they shall not go in to watch while the holy things are being covered, lest they die."*

The Bible nowhere indicates that Uzza was a Kohathite. If he was, what God did is even more understandable. Everyone in the whole procedure from David on down was guilty of disobeying God's instructions regarding the most holy things. David failed to consult with the High Priest - or any priest, for that matter - regarding how the Ark should be moved. Evidently, no priest protested that proper procedures were not being followed.

The Kohathites were not even supposed to look on the uncovered Ark. To God, when Uzzah reached out and touched the Ark as it seemed about to topple off the cart, it was no act of heroism but the final act of desecration, arrogance, and presumption.

The last thing presumed was that Uzza's hand was less defiling than the earth that he feared would contaminate the Ark.

God's instruction in Exodus 20:24-25 regards building Him an altar. An altar made for His worship had to be constructed of earth or unhewn stones. No altar defiled by man's sinful hand was suitable. Dirt cannot sin; it always follows the nature God established. God did not want the symbol of His throne contaminated by the evil that manifested itself in a whole string of rebellions against His specific instructions. There was nothing arbitrary, capricious, or whimsical in God's action.

Jesus teaches us to address God as "Father," a title suggesting familiarity, yet we are also to pray, "Hallowed be Your name." God shows in these two incidents that, if reverence is due to the symbols used in His worship, how much greater reverence must be given to the realities of the New Covenant?

Those involved in this incident were well-intentioned, but it illustrates for all generations that God still requires conformity with His directives concerning holy objects. Deviation from orthodoxy can be deadly.

### King Saul

Saul was not a great king, nor was he even a good man. He was deeply flawed. The entire first half of Samuel is dedicated to a character study about his failures. When reading through Samuel, you might have a tendency to become critical or judgmental of Saul at times. You will probably feel sorry for him at times too. But slow down and be honest with yourself. If you are open-minded, you will realize you likely have more in common with Saul than you would care to admit. The whole point of exploring Saul's failures is to warn us so we do not repeat his mistakes.

First Samuel offers up a number of illustrations, some seemingly small, some big, that examine Saul's missteps (see I Samuel:13-15). In essence, Saul's root character flaw is self-exaltation and self-deception. He thinks he knows better than everyone else, including God. The biggest tragedy is that he is not even aware of it. The story shows he is completely blind to his arrogance and always believes he is in the right.

### Eli's Sons

Eli was a devoted high priest who served forty years as judge of Israel, the first of priestly descent also to regulate the affairs of the people (see I Samuel 4:18; Bible Dictionary, "Eli," 663).

Eli was a good man who gave kind consideration to Hannah in her hour of great agony (see I Samuel, 1:1-18; 2:20-21) and paid careful attention to the upbringing and spiritual training of Hannah's son Samuel (see I Samuel 1:24-48; 2:18-26; 3:1-19).

Eli had two sons, Hophni and Phinehas. Together the three of them labored as priests at Shiloh in the tabernacle, where the ark of the covenant was housed (see I Samuel 1:3). In keeping with the requirements of the law of Moses, all Israelite males were required to appear before the Lord yearly on each of the great national festivals: Passover, Pentecost, and the Feast of the Tabernacles (see Bible Dictionary, "Feasts," 672–74). At Shiloh, Eli also officiated in the judgment seat (see I Samuel, 1:9). Hophni and Phinehas's role as priests was to function as mediators between God and His people in their worship and offering of sacrifices (see Bible Dictionary, "Priests," 753–54).

"Now the sons of Eli were sons of Belial; they knew not the Lord" (I Samuel 2:12). The term Belial means "worthless" or "wicked" (see Bible Dictionary, "Belial," 620). They were men of greed and lust. They used their authority as priests to extort from the people the best of the meat brought before them for sacrifice (I Samuel 2:13-16). In essence they were taking their portion before giving a portion to God. They were also committing immoral acts with the women who gathered at the tabernacle (I Samuel 2:22). Eli knew what they were doing, and when the people saw that the priesthood at Shiloh was corrupt, they "abhorred the offering of the Lord" (I Samuel 2:17). What was a father to do?

Eli confronted his sons, "Why do ye such things? ... Nay, my sons; for it is no good report that I hear: ye make the Lord's people to transgress" (I Samuel 2:24). Hophni

38

and Phinehas ignored the pleading words of their father. They continued in their evil ways; Eli's warning was too late.

# Chapter III

# Orphanism

The state of being an orphan carries with it a plethora of spiritual and psychological issues that tend to go unrecognized and therefore unaddressed, many of which I have personally experienced. For years I was ignorant to its onset for me and that healing from its effect was even possible. Naturally and spiritually, orphanism carries about with it the weight of a backstory defined by trauma, abandonment, abuse, or neglect. While not everyone is affected by orphanism naturally, we all have been affected by it spiritually. When the serpent tempted Eve in the Garden and she convinced her husband, Adam, to also partake in sharing the forbidden fruit, sin entered the world, the orphan spirit was unleashed, and all of mankind has suffered its effects.

Orphanism cause one to develop a false mindset that does not line up with the truth in God's Word. This spirit is false belief system put in place by the enemy. The Word of God says in Ephesians 1:6 that we are accepted in the beloved. So, it is a lie and deception from the enemy causing us to feel unaccepted. Please take the time to open your heart and get a revelation of God's love for you and change the direction of your bloodline back to fellowship with God. Allow him to heal and cleanse your heart. This could be your missing link to freedom. (Moore, n.d.)

### *What is its origin?*

Almost immediately after the fall in Eden, the fruit of this orphan spirit resulted in jealousy, culminating in Cain murdering his brother Abel because God the Father did not receive Cain's offering. (Genesis 4) To make matters worse, in today's society, with the breakup and perversion of God's design for marriages and families, large amounts of people are not only alienated from God but are brought up without the loving care and security of their biological fathers.

I believe all of the emotional, physical and spiritual troubles of society can be traced to humans feeling alienated from God and their biological fathers. Unhealed, orphaned men have a hard time connecting to their spouses, their children, those in spiritual authority and their supervisors, and they have a hard time accepting and loving themselves. There are presently too many incarcerated men who are acting out lives of violence and rebellion because their earthly fathers abandoned them. There are churches filled with pastors

42

and leaders who use people and destroy relationships because they are driven to succeed, and it is due to their need for a father's affirmation—which is a hole too large for ministry success or performance to fill. Far too many women today only find fulfillment in being complemented on their outward appearance and are unaccepting of the way they are formed and the One who formed them, causing aesthetic procedures and surgeries to be at an all-time high.

The only way to break this orphan spirit is for people to be filled with a sense of the Father's love for them in Christ, which then enables them to become mature sons and daughters who serve God out of knowledge of His undeserved grace instead of trying to earn the Father's love through performance. It will take spiritual parents with great spiritual depth and authority to break and reverse this curse to perpetuate a generational blessing. Again, only when a person is healed of fatherlessness through the love of God is the orphan spirit broken so they can begin the process of entering mature sonship. Sonship is so important that all creation is presently crying out for the manifestation of the mature sons of God (Romans 8:19)

# Chapter IV

## Fruit of the Orphan Spirit vs. the Fruit of the Holy Spirit

The enemy is known to be a mimic. It is his goal to deceive man with counterfeits. In this instance, just as the Holy Spirit bears fruit, so to the orphan spirit. Let's take a look at the following and contrast the two:

### *Insecurity*
The orphan spirit operates out of insecurity and jealousy. The spirit of sonship operates in love and acceptance.

Those with an orphan spirit are constantly battling jealousy and insecurity since security originates in a secure relationship with our parents. That has been one of the hardest struggles of my life, especially after having found out that I was being not raised by my biological dad. To make matters worse, Daddy, the man who was raising me was only there part-time. So, when I was being teased by family members, classmates, and other neighborhood kids, I felt more and more unworthy and unloved day by day. I was the skinny little nappy-headed girl with bucked teeth that was joned on in and outside of the family. Because I longed for acceptance so much, I began to behave very promiscuously throughout my teenage years and well into my twenties. My best girlfriends were very shapely, and seemingly had all of the things that boys and men desired, so I thought I had to show them up by any means necessary so that I would no longer be counted out because I did look like or have what they did.

Those with an orphan spirit are so insecure, they even have a hard time hearing a biological or spiritual father praise their siblings or co-laborers. When I received complements, it was, and sometimes still is hard for me to believe that they are coming from a sincere place. This could be why a lot of women are sometimes so "catty", being deliberately hurtful to one another, unloving and unkind...because of their own insecurities. Many women find it difficult to complement another woman for fear that it will take something away from them. I struggled with that for the greater part of my life before I found out who I was in Christ Jesus.

On the contrary, those with the spirit of sonship are so secure in the Father's love and favor that they are content to serve in any capacity needed, whether or not they are in charge or celebrated in the process. While leadership is a gift that I have, I also came to realize that I had to learn how to follow in order to be a good leader.  I was so insecure that not being "in charge" was an insult to me.  It meant that I was not enough, less than, inadequate, unintelligent, inferior.  In my relationship with the Lord, however, I learned that He has a unique plan for my life, a plan to prosper me and not to harm me, plans to give me hope and a future. (Jeremiah 29:11)

### *Jealousy*

The orphan spirit is jealous of the success of his brothers.  I still remember the day that my aunt told me that I needed to be more like my best friend at the time.  We were in our teens and still in high school.  Unlike my mom, her mom allowed her to work after school.  That allowed her to save up some money and her mom helped her purchase her first car.   Man was that annoying to hear my aunt say.  I mean this girl was already absolutely beautiful, with gorgeous, long, thick hair, hazel eyes, and quit shapely.  Now, she has her own car to boot, and again, I was being put down by my family who did not care about the differences in our circumstances.  She only saw that I was not enough in her eyes.

The mature son is committed to the success of his brothers.  I carried a lot of mixed emotions and feelings towards the children that my dad helped raise with the other lady, especially the child that they had together, but unbeknownst to me at the time, the Lord was always guiding me to do right by them, especially her.  So much so that when she was faced with some challenges in her life because of some poor choices she made, she and her baby boy came to live with me for a while.  The only requirement that I had for her was that she either go to school to learn how to do something to start a career or get a job that would allow her to support her and her child. I sincerely wanted to see her successful in life, especially after having had many people and the Lord extend grace and mercy my way.

Those with an orphan spirit are happy when their brother fails because it makes them feel good about themselves. I wonder how often Christians think or say, "That's what they get!" Grandma used to say all the time, "God don't like ugly, and He ain't to fond of pretty either." I am reminded of these sayings because in my immaturity, I would laugh when others were crying. When those who once hurt me were now hurting, my flesh was so pleased with that outcome for their life. Coming into maturity and sonship, that laughter became more and more uncomfortable, and I turned more and more to prayer and interceding, offering help to get my brother or sister back on their feet.

That best friend from high school got married soon after I did (the first time). Everything about them was seemingly perfect. They came from perfect families, had perfect children, bought the perfect house and cars. He had the perfect career while she stayed home with the children until she went back to school and finished her degree. It was seemingly the whole picket fence and a dog situation until infidelity crept into their marriage and she could not present herself as perfect anymore. Wow, oh wow did I have a field day with that one. I was happy for a moment at her failure because perhaps now I could be seen. What a number the devil had done on me. I was celebrating her brokenness out of my own brokenness.

On the other hand, those with the spirit of sonship joyfully commit themselves to serve, celebrate and help their brothers succeed, since they don't work for human accolades but out of a deep sense of the love and affirmation of Father God.

When I first got saved, I attended a church in the community that I lived in. I was able to build relationships, genuine relationships with so many of the people there. A lot of the young women and girls and I really connected and developed a sisterhood. The bonds in those relationships are very strong today. So much so that one of the younger ladies and her new husband are now my Pastor and First Lady. With the leading of the Holy Spirit, I joined their ministry and serve under them. I support them whenever and wherever I am able. I knew that I was called to teach and preach the Word of God myself, but my initial assignment was to give my sister and her husband my support to help grow their ministry. I celebrate the elevation in her life, her relationship, and her ministry as she preaches, teaches, and leads the women (and men) that she is called to. In serving them as they began to elevate, the Lord elevated me.

### Serves God to Earn His Love
The orphan spirit serves God to earn the Father's love. The mature son serves God out of a sense of divine acceptance and favor. Along these lines, those with an orphan spirit are constantly striving and trying to earn the Father's love through accomplishment in ministry or career. Those with a spirit of sonship already know they

are accepted in Christ and serve others out of the abundance of this acceptance.

## Medicates Through Physical Stimulation

The orphan spirit tries to medicate its deep internal alienation through physical stimulation. The mature son walks in the joy and presence of the Lord for comfort. Those with an orphan spirit are constantly trying to push down their sense of alienation, loneliness and lack of self-worth through constant work, going from one relationship to the next, physical gratification and a life of narcissism and self-indulgence. However, the more they indulge, the more addicted they become and the larger the hole in their heart becomes because only the love of the Father can fill the deep emotional needs they have. Those walking in sonship, however, bask in the presence and love of God and practice the joy of the Lord continually as their source of strength because they understand that grounding their security and self-life in anything other than God is like trying to build a house on sinking sand.

## Driven by the Need for Success

The orphan spirit is driven by the need for success. The Holy Spirit leads the mature son into his calling and mission. Many attempt to accomplish great things to satisfy the deep yearning in their hearts for their father's approval. This results in them being driven to succeed instead of being led by the Spirit. Even many leaders get their churches into huge debt to build huge buildings, driving the people around them because they are blinded by their own innate feelings of inadequacy. They think they can feel good about themselves with great accomplishments.

Only those with a strong sense of sonship will allow the Lord to direct them and bring opportunities to them without trying to drum up their own success.

## Uses People as Objects to Fulfill Their Goals

The orphan spirit uses people as objects to fulfill goals. Mature sons serve people to bless the kingdom. Those with an orphan spirit tend to use people as objects to accomplish their goals. Whenever we objectify people, we manipulate them with words threats, and anything necessary to have our way and control them. Mature people who walk in sonship don't use people; they serve and release people to fulfill their destiny in Christ.

## Repels Their Children

Leaders and parents with an orphan spirit are constantly in turmoil, fighting and striving for their own way, which gives their spiritual children the sense that their leader is in competition with them instead of loving them. This results in repelling spiritual and biological children, which can forfeit influence over the next generation. Those who walk in sonship walk in the Father's anointing and draw children toward them because their children hear the voice of a shepherd who cares for them.

## Has an Issue with Anger and Fits of Rage

The orphan spirit has anger and fits of rage. The spirit of sonship rests in the Father's ability to control and guide the future. Those with an orphan spirit have issues with uncontrollable anger, fits of rage and other forms of manipulation because they feel they must control others and their circumstances in order to fulfill their goals. This is because they lack the trust necessary in their heavenly Father to guide and control their future. Those walking in sonship walk in the Father's rest and have ceased from their own works so the Father can have His way in their lives.

### Always in Competition with Others

The orphan spirit is always in competition with others. The spirit of sonship is always blessing others. Those with an orphan spirit are always trying to outdo others in their church, family, business or denomination because they receive their identity through being better than everyone else. Those who walk in sonship are constantly seeing how they can bless others, since they already have the affirmation of God in their souls. They want to freely share His love with others.

### Lacks Self-Esteem

The orphan spirit lacks self-esteem. The spirit of sonship walks in the love and acceptance of Father God. Those with an orphan spirit have a hard time loving and accepting themselves. Those walking in sonship are filled with a sense of divine love and acceptance that enables them to walk confidently in the joy of the Lord in spite of the fact that all humans are sinners and fall short of the glory of God. (Romans 3:23)

### Materialistic

The orphan spirit receives its primary identity through material possessions, physical appearance, and activities. The spirit of sonship is grounded in the Father's affirmation. Those with an orphan spirit never have enough career success, material possessions, pleasure, or illicit relationships to satisfy the hole in their heart related to their identity.    Consequently, they are constantly striving to gain satisfaction through the use of various things or people in their lives. In many cases, even their form of dress—including an inordinate amount of tattoos, skin piercings and hairdos—can be their way of standing out as unique in a cry for attention due to a lack of self-esteem and fatherly affirmation.

Those who walk in sonship are so grounded in their heavenly Father's affirmation that they can be satisfied serving in the background and can celebrate the success and attention others receive.  The void in their soul has already been filled with the unconditional love of the Father.

The greatest gift known to humankind is to accept, receive and walk in the love of the Father, who so loved the world that He gave His only begotten Son so that we may not perish or waste our lives away but experience the abundant life that only our divine Father can give. (John 3:16) (Mattera, n.d.)

# Chapter V

## The First Orphan

The orphan spirit is a demonic spirit that was introduced by Satan, the destroyer, murderer, and liar. The great irony of it all is that this same spirit was released to the world through one man, Adam, the son of God (see Luke 3:38; and Romans 5:12). The devil was and will always be the first orphan. His primary goal is to turn everyone into versions of himself - fatherless, disinherited, and lost.

Can you imagine once being God's beloved and being the ultimate insider to now having to be on the outside looking in, watching everything that was going on in the garden through envious eyes and an insecure heart, watching as the happy family of God took a stroll together according to Genesis chapter three? Before he became Satan, lucifer was an archangel who had the same degree of importance as Gabriel, the messenger, and as Michael, the warrior. Unfortunately, Lucifer thought he could be like God. He became corrupt thinking that he and 1/3 of heaven's angels could defeat the forces of God. Pride came before the great fall. It led to his delusion in declaring his exaltation above God (Isaiah 14:13-14).

The most important thing to the devil was and continually will be himself. In contrast, Jesus spent time on His knees in pray, careful not to make any decisions without consulting the will of His Father. Jesus had the heart of a son and was careful to stay in alignment with His will. The orphan spirit, however, resists the Father's love. For clarity, let us look deeper at that passage of Scripture to examine several issues of "self" that led to Satan's fall.

### Self-Will
Lucifer became the devil because he was headstrong and did not care what the Father had to say about his plans and activities. He arrogantly declared, "I will ascend to heaven." What a familiar, self-centered mindset and spirit that many of us have, or have had. We often see this tendency to do whatever they want to do in children, regardless of what their father may think, and without regard to whether it will bring happiness or sorrow.

### Self-Exaltation
Lucifer wanted to be higher than God saying, "I will set my throne above God's stars." This rebellious spirit is in direct opposition to the Spirit of Jesus, who happily came under submission to the will of the Father. Jesus

was willing to submit even to the point of death (see Luke 22:42).

## Self-Enthronement

Wanting to rule the earth, Lucifer arrogantly declared, "I will set my throne...". God wants to be Lord over all the earth, and that includes our lives, because He knows He is the only one who can rule righteously. When the children of Adam, carrying the orphan spirit, were scattered all over the planet, they wanted to build their own kingdoms and their own systems of governance, without considering if they were in alignment with their father in heaven. They are a perfect example of the orphan mind, which has a belief system that insists it can do a much better job than God.

Satan, in his foolishness, brought Jesus to a high peak and showed him the kingdoms of the world. Satan said he would give all of those kingdoms to Him if the Son of God would bow down and worship him. Jesus responded to him with one of the most powerful weapons ever, the Word of God, saying, "Away from Me, Satan! For it is written: 'Worship the Lord your God and serve him only'" (Matthew 4:10).

## Self-Deification

Lastly, Lucifer said, "I will make myself like the Most-High." (New International Version). Instead of saying "Thy will be done", he said "I will", which is the highest form of self-glorification. Again, this is in direct contrast to Jesus' attitude, which pleased the Father because He was willing to be under the Father's authority. Our attitude should be the same as that of Jesus Christ's: *Who, being in very nature God, did not consider equality with God something to be used to his own advantage; rather, He made Himself nothing by taking the very nature of a servant, being made in human likeness. And being found in appearance as a man, He humbled Himself and became obedient to death—even death on a cross!* (Philippians 2:5-8) (Hetland, 2020)

"The thief comes only to steal and kill and destroy. I came that they may have life and have it more abundantly."
*John 10:10 ESV*

# Chapter VI

# Heart Condition

*Keep thy heart with all diligence; for out of it are the issues of life.*
*Proverbs 4:23*

Even after having heard the truth from my mom about who my biological father was, the only emotion I was able to readily identify and attach to what I was feeling was rejection, but I still could not connect that feeling of rejection to my behavior and choices at that time.

Most of us have heard of separation anxiety. It is a real thing. When a baby is separated from its parents, it oftentimes experiences great fear. This is actually a normal reaction when those who they have known as protectors are no longer with them.

The same was true when man chose to turn their backs on God, an unexpected fear entered their lives. Their protector and provider *appeared* to have left their presence. The thing we must know about God is that He is merciful. So often, when we have done something wrong, we take the way of Adam and Eve and recoil—isolating ourselves from God and others. We feel alienated and alone. But the opposite is true. God never leaves us... we leave Him.

I have learned that God is a gentleman. He will never violate our decisions, even when they may go against His greatest desire—to draw near to us. When a wrong decision is made it is good to know that He is quick to forgive, if we will only come to Him.

There is something unique about a father's role in the life of a child. The father and child relationship is the heart of where our identity is formed, and it should be a healthy picture of how our Heavenly Father interacts with us. When one is abandoned or rejected by their earthly father, a deep void is created. This often makes it difficult for us to interact with our God. Our trust has been broken, and healing must take place.

Knowing the Father's love is very important and necessary for a Believer to function as a healthy member of the Body of Christ. Again, what does an orphan spirit look like? A type of demonic spirit that invades a person's mind causing a sense of abandonment, loneliness, alienation, and isolation. It often attaches itself to someone who has experienced extreme rejection in his or her life. A person operating out of an orphan spirit compensates these feelings of insecurities by being performance driven, competitive, and works independently. They struggle with self-worth and find it difficult to maintain healthy relationships.

We often live with dysfunction for such a long time in our lives, that we don not realize we are struggling.

Ask yourself these questions...

- Do I operate out of insecurity?
- Am I jealous of others' successes?
- Do I serve God to earn His love?
- Do I self-medicate by pulling deeply inward?
- Do I struggle with self-worth?
- Do I fill the void by working constantly, through physical gratification, or with narcissistic behavior and/or self-indulgence?
- Am I driven by the need to succeed?
- Do I use people to accomplish my goals?
- Do I repel my biological or spiritual children?
- Do I struggle with anger or fits of rage?
- Am I always in competition with others?
- Do I lack self-esteem?
- Do I receive my identity from material possessions, physical appearance, or activities?

If you've answered yes to several of these, it is safe to say that maybe there is a heart issue that is deeply in need of healing. To get to that place of healing, we have to go from abandoned to adopted. You see the opposite of one abandoned is one adopted, and adoption is a very beautiful thing.

When a child is adopted, they are no longer penniless. They are no longer without a name. They are, in the best of scenarios, given an identity through a new family—where they will be loved and appreciated. Often, in cases of adoption, the family they are given, provides much better care than the original parents ever could. When we are operating in the spirit of adoption...

- We are secure
- We celebrate the accomplishments of others
- We experience acceptance
- We fill emotional voids with intimate time with the Father
- We allow the Spirit to lead us into our calling
- We serve others and provide opportunities for them to grow in their own destiny in Christ
- We don't use anger or other forms of manipulation to get our way
- We bless others around us, freely sharing the Father's love with others
- We love ourselves and exhibit healthy self-esteem
- We are grounded in our identity in Christ

How do I get healing from something that has controlled my life for so long?
The first step to healing is admitting that there is a problem in the first place.
Now, I want to tell you this is a lifestyle change. It is easy to pray a simple prayer, but the next steps are sometimes more difficult. When we make changes in our life it takes courage and often self-discipline.

I encourage you during this time of healing to write in a journal about what the Holy Spirit is showing you. For example, if anger and rage begin to creep in, I strongly recommend that you take time to slow down and evaluate the open door. Are you feeling rejected in that moment? Are you wanting your way, and pushing to get it? Ask the Holy Spirit to reveal the Lord's truth about the situation.

Look to the Word of God...Here are several scriptures that I recommend as you continue to work through battling in the opposite spirit, the spirit of adoption:

> "There is one who speaks like the piercings of a sword, but the tongue of the wise promotes health."—Proverbs 12:18

> "Even so the tongue is a little member and boasts great things. See how great a forest a little fire kindles!"—James 3:5

> "Every good gift and every perfect gift is from above, and comes down from the Father of lights, with whom there is no variation or shadow of turning."—James 1:7

*"Be anxious for nothing, but in everything by prayer and supplication, with thanksgiving, let your requests be made known to God."*—Philippians 4:6

*"Likewise, the Spirit also helps in our weaknesses. For we do not know what we should pray for as we ought, but the Spirit Himself makes intercession for us with groanings which cannot be uttered. Now He who searches the hearts knows what the mind of the Spirit is, because He makes intercession for the saints according to the will of God."*—Romans 8:26-27

*"And He said, 'My Presence will go with you, and I will give you rest.'"*—Exodus 33:14

*"Commit your works to the Lord, and your thoughts will be established."*—Proverbs Chapter sixteen, verse three

*"For I know the thoughts that I think toward you, says the Lord, thoughts of peace and not of evil, to give you a future and a hope."*—Jeremiah Chapter twenty-nine, verse eleven

*"For God is not the author of confusion but of peace, as in all the churches of the saints."*—First Corinthians, Chapter thirteen, verse thirty-three

*"But as it is written: 'Eye has not seen, nor ear heard, nor have entered into the heart of man the things which God has prepared for those who love Him.'"*—1 Corinthians 2:9

*"You will also declare a thing, and it will be established for you; so light will shine on your ways."*—Job 22:28

*"But if you have bitter envy and self-seeking in your hearts, do not boast and lie against the truth. This wisdom does not descend from above, but is earthly, sensual, demonic. For where envy and self-seeking exist, confusion and every evil thing are there."*—James 3:14-16

*"Let nothing be done through selfish ambition or conceit, but in lowliness of mind let each esteem others better than himself."*—Philippians 2:3

67

*"For you have need of endurance, so that after you have done the will of God, you may receive the promise."*—Hebrews 10:36

I want to encourage you in the Lord. If today you have found that you are struggling with the orphan spirit, please know that there should be no shame in this. We have all battled it at one point or another—some of us more than others, depending on the level of rejection or abandonment we have experienced in our lives.

It is my desire to see the Body of Christ healed and walking in their true purposes in Jesus Christ. I declare a blessing over you in the name of Jesus as you continue to do Kingdom work, walking in your true identity as a loved son or daughter of the Most-High God.

# Part II:
# The Spirit of Adoption

# Chapter VII

# The Spirit of Adoption

*For you did not receive the spirit of bondage again to*
*fear,*
*but you received the Spirit of adoption, by whom we*
*cry out,*
*"Abba, Father."*
*Romans 8:15 NKJV*

Adoption is the act or process of taking someone or something by choice into a relationship. More specifically, it is taking a child born to other parents voluntarily as one's own child, especially in compliance with formal legal procedures. Whether it is a family with fertility difficulties which causes them to resort to some other means by which to become parents, or just the opposite, a couple who wants to add to their family despite already having children, a single woman or man who wants to be a parent, Little Orphan Annie, children in foreign countries, or children left behind in hospitals...there is one commonality for them all. The children in each of these scenarios were somehow separated from one or both of their parents and have therefore become orphans. My personal adoption story is no different.

The thought of being "adopted" as I had heard about and seen on television was vastly different than what my experience was, yet there is still some commonality in that I experienced separation from my biological parent and was taken into relationship by choice by my adopted dad.

Our Heavenly Father never intended for us to live as orphans without a Father, or without a home. His plan even before creation was to have a family. He created a son, Adam, and gave him the perfect home and desired for him to rule in the authority given to him by his Father God. Then the enemy came to kill, steal, and destroy all that Father God had intended. Father God restored us back to Himself through His son Jesus, yet many of us still live as orphans trying to work for our inheritance and the right to be in the Father's house. The orphan spirit cannot be cast out; it can only be displaced by love because perfect love cast out all fear. I John 4:18

All that Father God has is ours! All creation is groaning for the sons and daughters to be revealed. It is time for us to come into the fullness of who we were created to be so all creation will come back to the Father's house. In this eighth chapter of the Apostle Paul's message to the Church in Rome, he is comforting the people of God.

By grace, God has done everything necessary to bring us back into relationship with Him. In Ephesians 1:4-5, Paul writes that God, IN LOVE, planned our ADOPTION. In love he predestined us for adoption as sons through Jesus Christ, according to the purpose of his will, to the praise of his glorious grace, with which he has blessed us in the Beloved. God's plan for adoption implies something about who we became in our sin—ORPHANS. Having inherited a sinful nature from our first parents (Adam and Eve), we willfully and joyfully pursued our own fleshly desires, and became CHILDREN OF WRATH following the course of this world. In rebellion, we ran away from our true Father and chose to live as orphans in the DEVIL'S ADOPTION AGENCY...like the rest of mankind.

An orphan is, by definition, a child who has been deprived of parental love, protection, and care. Usually, this is the result of death. Spiritually speaking, death came into the world because of sin. Therefore, just as sin came into the world through one man, and death through sin, and so death spread to all men because all sinned (Romans 5:12). SIN MADE US ORPHANS, and every orphan desires in their heart to be adopted. Every orphan has a deep-rooted longing to be accepted and loved. In other words, everyone is struggling for validation—because no one really feels worthy. As we live in the world, which is really an adoption agency for the devil, men seek different "fathers", saviors who they believe will rescue us from those feelings of worthlessness. None are found because there are none to find.

1. Orphans are FATHERLESS - Orphans are uncertain of who they are—they have no identity—no one to tell them who they are. Without an identity, they seek to find it in what they do, what they have achieved, what they have done right, what they have done wrong, or what others think of them.

2. Orphans are UNDISCIPLINED - Orphans are weak and defenseless. They are vulnerable to negative influence and unrestrained passions because there is no one devoted to their loving protection.

3. Orphans are FEARFUL - Orphans live in fear of rejection, enslaved to performance. They are never sure if they are good enough. Every time we make a mistake or fall short of an expectation, we feel great dread.

4. Orphans are ALONE - Orphans do not have family. This often leads them to build communities with other orphans just as messed up as they are. There they are affirmed but never healed.

5. Orphans are BITTER - Orphans can live believing they deserve and are entitled to more. They are not responsible for their mistakes, failures, or

current situation. They are victims of people, institutions, and circumstances.

6. Orphans are INSECURE - Orphans live and measure their lives according to how we compare with others. They compete with others for approval. They are, therefore, unable to love others or rejoice with others easily. Instead, they exist in a constant state of feeling inferior or superior to others.

7. Orphans are HOPELESS - Orphans live without a certain future. They ultimately do not know what is going to happen tomorrow, let alone in eternity. Sin made us orphans – WE HAD NO FATHER. Spiritual orphans live with a spiritual sadness—an undeniable and unavoidable state of feeling unworthy, unwanted, and unaccepted. In truth, men in their flesh ARE unlovable and unworthy.

Our adoption files are twelve inches thick. They are full of our crimes, our personality weaknesses, our character flaws, and more. Each of our files is an encyclopedia of sin we committed and love we omitted. It lists what is broken in us, what is deficient in us, and what is rebellious in us. No one in their right mind would want to bring you into their home, into their family. In the hours before He would be arrested and sentenced to die, Jesus said to His disciples: *"I will not leave you as orphans; I will come to you. Yet a little while and the world will see me no more, but you will see me. Because I live, you also will live. John 14:18*

## *Justification*

God reclaims us God did not need us, but He wanted us. That is the GRACE of adoption. But our adoption price is infinitely high. God cannot bring us into the family in our present condition. His holiness and perfection require that we have a perfect record. To live with God, our adoption file must be expunged, we must have more than a CLEAN record; we need a PERFECT record. Jesus chose to love us in our ungodliness.

> *For while we were still weak, at the right time Christ died for the ungodly. For one will scarcely die for a righteous person— though perhaps for a good person one would dare even to die - but God shows his love for us in that while we were still sinners, Christ died for us. Romans 5:6 - 8*

Before the foundation of the world, God planned our adoption. Through adoption, God reclaims (CALLS) His children back to Himself and admits them into his family. Ephesians 1:6 says, this adoption takes place THROUGH JESUS CHRIST.

> *And those whom he predestined he also called, and those whom he called he also justified, and those whom he justified he also glorified. Romans 8:30*

Justification makes adoption possible. What was necessary for our justification? John Stott explains that,

76

*"Justification is a legal term borrowed from the law courts. It is the exact opposite of 'condemnation" (cf. Deut.25:1; Prov.17:15; Rom.8:33-34). 'To condemn' is to declare somebody guilty; 'to justify' is to declare him righteous. In the Bible it refers to God's act of unmerited favor by which He puts a sinner right with Himself, not only pardoning or acquitting him, but accepting and treating him as righteous."*

*For God has done what the law, weakened by the flesh, could not do. By sending his own Son in the likeness of sinful flesh and for sin, He condemned sin in the flesh, in order that the righteous requirement of the law might be fulfilled in us, who walk not according to the flesh but according to the Spirit. Romans 8:3-4*

OUR JUSTIFICATION MEANS THREE THINGS:

1. Legal Exoneration: WE ARE DECLARED INNOCENT!! Justification - just-as-if-I-did not.

   • God forgives past sin. - For as high as the heavens are above the earth, so great is his steadfast love toward those who fear him; as far as the east is from the west, so far does he remove our transgressions from us. Psalm 103:11-12

   • God forgives present sin. There is therefore NOW no condemnation for those who are in Christ Jesus. Romans 8:1

   • God forgives future sin. My little children, I am writing these things to you so that you may not sin. But if anyone does sin, we have an advocate with the Father, Jesus Christ the righteous. I John 2:1

2.  Legal Union: WE ARE DECLARED RIGHTEOUS

- We are given Christ's life and Christ takes my death. It is more than just getting out of prison; it is like receiving *The Congressional Medal of Honor.*

- We are given Christ's perfect record. We are treated as if we lived a perfect life that Jesus lived.

- We are given the love that Jesus deserved - a legal and personal UNION is created.

- We are given all of this by faith. Christ is the grounds for our righteousness. We are not declared righteous because of our faith. Our faith is always impure. We are not saved by the quantity or quality of our faith, but by the object of our faith. Faith declares that only Christ saves and only Christ justifies. FAITH IS TRUSTING CHRIST DOES IT ALL.

But when the goodness and loving kindness of God our Savior appeared, He saved us, not because of works done by us in righteousness, but according to His own mercy, by the washing of regeneration and renewal of the Holy Spirit, whom he poured out on us richly through Jesus Christ our Savior, so that being justified by His grace we might become heirs according to the hope of eternal life. Titus 3:4-7

3. Legal Empowerment: WE ARE DECLARED BLESSED

- We are blessed. We no longer have to fear we are too bad to deserve God's love.
- We are blessed. We no longer have to perform to get God's love.
- We are blessed. We can approach God like a Father for love.
- We are blessed. We are freed from comparing and compete with others.
- We are blessed. We are part of a family.
- We are blessed. We enjoy the security of a guaranteed future.
- We are blessed. We delight in God as our loving Father who delights in us.

Christians, like orphans, do not always live in the joy of their justification—this is the reason for much of their pride and spiritual deadness. They continue to live like fear-filled orphans, uncertain of God's love who believe that their position with God is dependent upon the quality of their behavior and the purity of their hearts. We don't have to live in that kind of fear. The cross is God's declaration that I love you.

There is no fear in love, but perfect love casts out fear. For fear has to do with punishment, and whoever fears has not been perfected in love. I John 4:18

We have gone from *orphans* to *sons(daughters)*. If God loves you like that as an evil child, how much more then as HIS SON(DAUGHTER). We base what we do on who we are in Christ, our practice on our position, not our position on our practice. If you believe that you are accepted only because of your obedience, you will live like an orphan forever uncertain of God's love. You will remain prideful, fearful, performance driven, comparison-focused, and radically insecure, but when you believe *I AM ACCEPTD,* you will live a life of peace, love, and gratitude. Children of God do not obey to be accepted, yet because we are accepted, reciprocally, we obey.

To summarize, reclaiming our obedience is our response to God's gracious love. The symbol of Christianity is a Roman torture device. We can try to explain away many of the difficulties and sharp edges of God, but we will always come back to the violent death of Jesus Christ on the cross as the centerpiece of our faith. Even more thought provoking is that God designed it this way.

> And all that dwell upon the earth shall worship him, whose names are not written in the book of life of the Lamb slain from the foundation of the world. *Revelation 13:8 (KJV)*

If God was chosen to go through all of this, then it must have been because there was something accomplished there that could not be done in any other way. In pursuit of His own glory, God's focus was always on us. He is not selfish - He is utterly selfless. In love, Jesus was willing to put Himself to shame and extreme pain in order to secure our redemption. Our adoption is not only our exoneration of our spiritual poverty, but also our invitation to enjoy the riches of God's grace.

Do you believe God loves you? In our pain, loss, failure, weakness, mistakes...God loves us! He loves us before we are good. He loves us even though we are bad. He never stops loving us - the Holy Spirit is the seal of our adoption.

*There is therefore now no condemnation for those who are in Christ Jesus. For the law of the Spirit of life has set you free in Christ Jesus from the law of sin and death. For God has done what the law, weakened by the flesh, could not do. By sending his own Son in the likeness of sinful flesh and for sin, he condemned sin in the flesh, in order that the righteous requirement of the law might be fulfilled in us, who walk not according to the flesh but according to the Spirit. For those who live according to the flesh set their minds on the things of the flesh, but those who live according to the Spirit set their minds on the things of the Spirit. For to set the mind on the flesh is death, but to set the mind on the Spirit is life and 5 peace. For the mind that is set on the flesh is hostile to God, for it does not submit to God's law; indeed, it cannot. Those who are in the flesh cannot please God. You, however, are not in the flesh but in the Spirit, if in fact the Spirit of God dwells in you. Anyone who does not have the Spirit of Christ does not belong to him. But if Christ is in you, although the body is dead because of sin, the Spirit is life because of righteousness. If the Spirit of him who raised Jesus from the dead dwells in you, he who raised Christ Jesus from the dead will also give life to your mortal bodies through his Spirit who dwells in you. So then, brothers, we are debtors, not to the flesh, to live according to the flesh. For if you live according to the flesh you will die, but if by the Spirit you put to death the deeds of the body, you will live. For all who are led by the Spirit of God are sons of God. For you did not receive the spirit of slavery to fall back into fear, but you have received the Spirit of adoption as sons, by whom we cry, "Abba! Father!" The Spirit himself bears witness with our spirit that we are children of God, and if children, then heirs—heirs of God and fellow heirs with Christ, provided we suffer with him in order that we may also be glorified with him. (Romans 8:1-18)*

# Chapter VIII

# Rights As a Daughter of God

"The Spirit of the Lord is upon me, because he hath anointed me to preach the gospel to the poor; he hath sent me to heal the broken hearted, to preach deliverance to the captives, and recovery of sight to the blind, to set at liberty them that are bruised."
Luke 4:18

## *Liberty in Christ*

In the above scripture, the word liberty means "release"; in other words, "to set free" or "to bring out of slavery." Jesus said that the Spirit of the Lord had anointed Him to set men free, to release those who were bruised. This gives us an idea of what liberty is. Take a closer look at some other scriptures where the word is used will give more insight into its meaning and importance.

"For, brethren, ye have been called unto liberty; only use not liberty for an occasion to the flesh, but by love serve one another." (Galatians 5:13) Paul says, "You have been called unto liberty." The original word from which "liberty" as used in Galatians 5:13 was translated right, which is different from that used in Luke 4:18. "Liberty" in Galatians 5:13 implies the same as in Galatians 2:4 where Paul said: "And that because of false brethren unawares brought in, who came in privily to spy out our liberty which we have in Christ Jesus, that they might bring us into bondage:" The word "liberty" in this verse of scripture actually means the same thing as "right" (as in one's right). It is synonymous with authority, but in this case, it emphasizes a right: a legal right! When he says we have been called unto liberty (Galatians 5:13), he means we have been called into freedom, the kind of freedom that empowers one with a legal right.

Combining this meaning of liberty with that of Luke 4:18, provides better understanding of the word "liberty." This means that Christ brought us out of slavery, so He could bring us into freedom: freedom with legal rights. Now, it is one thing to bring someone out of something, and it is another to bring him into something else. Jesus brought us out so He could bring us in. We have therefore been called unto liberty in Christ. We have been brought out of slavery and brought into freedom. And in that liberty, we have rights. In talking about liberty in Christ, we are also talking about the rights we have in Christ:

- The right to choose
- The right to live
- The right to ask for what is yours
- The right to rule

## The Right to Choose

One thing about Jesus that a lot of people do not know is that He gives to everyone who comes to Him the right to choose. Christianity is not a religion. In the religions of the world, you lose your right to choose, and as a matter of fact, you almost lose your personality. You become a religious and psychological nonperson. You lose the right to choose to whoever or whatever is extolled to be "god." You cannot choose what you want anymore. Somehow, this opinion of religion has been passed from one generation to another, and people have come to think that God is really like that. They think that you lose yourself when you come to Jesus. They think, "Well, if I am born again, I will not be able to do what I want to do. I will lose my right to choose." God forbid! Yet, it is sad to note that some Christians have helped in perpetuating this erroneous idea because of the way they present Christianity to the world. When you come to Jesus, He gives you the right to choose. Sometimes, though, people have not been able to choose for fear of missing out on God's will for them.

I recently heard a story of a young lady who said a guy came to her and said she was to be his wife according to the ordinance of God. This guy said that God had spoken to him and said he was to marry her, and she felt terrible. She felt terrible because she believed she was supposed to marry him, and she did not want to. It seemed to her that she could not do anything about it. She prayed, asking God why He would do such a thing to her, telling her to marry someone she did not want for a husband. She respected the gentleman because he was a good preacher. He also obviously knew how to talk the young lady into believing it was God's will. Then one day, she heard a preacher say something from the Bible, that a lady is free to be married to whomsoever she wishes. She was surprised and asked if the Bible really said so. She demanded that to be shown where it was in Scripture. When she saw it in the Bible, she exclaimed, "Wow!" No one knew what her trouble was until she told the preacher all about it. She had been bound. She thought she could not make a choice because God had handed her a husband.

A lot of people are like that. They say, "If God says that is who you are going to marry, then that is who you must marry. Or if you do not get that job, no matter how good it is, then it means God does not want you to have the good job." *"God says...God says...God says..."* until we become "nobodies." When Jesus came, He showed us that things were not that way. You do have a right to choose. Life really begins when you give your life to your Creator and He gives you the power to face reality. This is the good life.

In Mark 10, we find a beautiful story of a blind man named Bartimaeus. He always sat by the roadside begging for alms. Then one day, while he was there begging in his usual manner, Jesus Christ passed by. Blind Bartimaeus heard the noise and called to someone to tell him what was going on. They told him, "Jesus of Nazareth is passing by." The Bible says he began to cry out loud, "Jesus, Son of David, have mercy on me." There was a crowd with Jesus and quite a number of them were in front of him, and when they got to where blind Bartimaeus was, they told him to hold his peace.

According to their *religion*, if you were sick or blind, then it was seen as God being against you. In other words, the sickness was a reflection of your sin, in which case, you had no right to healing. This meant you could not dare ask for healing. So, they said to him, "Stop! Do not talk anymore. The Master is coming. Be quiet!" But praise God, the Bible says Bartimaeus yelled the louder, "Jesus, Son of David, have mercy on me." The Bible goes on to say that when Jesus Christ got to him, He stopped and asked for him to be brought to Him. Blind Bartimaeus was brought face to face with Jesus. Then, Jesus asked him a question: "...What wilt thou that I should do unto thee?" (Mark 10:51). That means, what do you want me to do for you? Jesus gave him the right to choose. Did you see that? He was ready to do anything, whatever blind Bartimaeus wanted.

Many people are not yet at that point in their lives where they have made a decision concerning what they want from God, because religion tells them not to ask God for anything. They have been told that God has no time to spend on them and their meagre thoughts or desires. "God, Who is Almighty, and you, so insignificant," they say. So, religion has told them that regardless of what their present state is, it is God's will for them. A man who is born deaf in one ear is so because that is God's will for him. To the poor, they say, "That's how it has been in your family lineage: poverty belongs to you. It is God's way of keeping your family humble." And so, many people have been defeated psychologically because of the lack of knowledge. They do not really know who God is.

Another time, Jesus was walking along a street in Jerusalem with His disciples, and they came to a man who had been blind from birth (John 9:1-3). The disciples asked the Master questions regarding what they had been taught by the Scribes and Pharisees. They asked, "Master, who did sin, this man or his parents, that he was born blind?" Jesus answered and said: "None of them." To them, it flowed from their religious upbringing that if someone was born blind, then either he or his parents must have sinned. What a foolish question! How could he have sinned before he was born? But then, that was their mentality, and the Pharisees must have had an explanation for it. They taught the people that any situation they found themselves in was somehow ordained by God. But that is not true, for only good and perfect gifts come from God (James 1:17).

Another time, Jesus was at the pool of Bethesda where He saw a lot of sick people. There were people with all kinds of diseases there, a multitude of them. (John 5:1). The Bible recalls that when Jesus came to a man who had an infirmity for thirty-eight years, He asked if he wanted to be healed. That was great, right? The Pharisees would never have entertained that kind of desire. No one was supposed to ask for healing. How could they, when they reasoned that since God made them that way, they had to stay that way. Some people still say sickness is a way to glorify God.

A lady once said to a preacher: "God put the sickness on me to make me humble." The preacher responded, "Great! God needs many humble people," and he prayed, "Father, give her more of it so she can be humbler!" But she shouted, "No, I do not want more of it!" The preacher, faking surprise, asked, "But if this sickness is God's will for you, don't you want to have more of God's will?"

Religion binds people. It promises liberty, while it is itself a slave to human limitations. Religion reveals someone trying to reach out to God, to touch Him, to get something from Him, and get Him to do something. That is the kind of religion many people have. Unfortunately, such people think that is what Christianity is all about: trying to get God to do something. The Pharisees taught the people that way, but when Jesus came, He brought another message. He said, "God loves you. God wants to touch you."

There were so many rabbis in Israel, but this was one Rabbi that was so different. His message was different. All the other rabbis talked about reaching out to God, but this Rabbi came and said, "God has already done something for you; God loves you.", but their small minds could not handle this. Jesus asked, "What do you want me to do for you?" (Mark 10:51). "Do you want to be healed?" (John 5:6). He gave them the right to choose. When you come to Him, He does not destroy your personality. Instead, He puts power in your personality and makes you effective and influential. He loves you the way you are. When you come to Him, He takes away the sin nature and all that is associated with it, and He puts in you the desire and the ability to do right, and the freedom to choose. He sets you at liberty to serve God as you should. Glory to God!

## YOU CAN KNOW HIS WILL

Some people don't understand what it means to know the will of God. They say, "Well, I hope if it is the will of God, I will get the job." They always think that God's will is against them. They do not like to say what they want to do because they feel God may just not like it, but if you ask them what God likes, they will still be unable to say what it is. They have turned God into a mysterious being. Someone said, "God works in mysterious ways, His wonders to perform." God is not mysterious. To be mysterious means to be a "strange dude" that cannot be understood, and that is not who God is. He showed us His will by giving us His Word. He has told us what He did, what He is doing, and what He is going to do, so we can understand Him. He is neither strange nor mysterious. Yes, there was a mystery, but Jesus came to solve the mystery.

> *"In the body of his flesh through death, to present you holy and unblameable and unreproveable in his sight: If ye continue in the faith 'grounded and settled, and be not moved away from the hope of the gospel, which ye have heard, and which was preached to every creature which is under heaven; whereof I Paul am made a minister; Who now rejoice in my sufferings for you, and fill up that which is behind of the afflictions of Christ in my flesh for his body's sake, which is the*

*church: Whereof I am made a minister, according to the dispensation of God which is given to me for you, to fulfil the word of God; Even the MYSTERY which hath been hid from ages and from generations, but now is made manifest to his saints: To whom God would make known what is the riches of the glory of this MYSTERY among the Gentiles; which is Christ in you, the hope of glory:"*
*Colossians 1:22-27*

Paul, speaking by the inspiration of the Holy Spirit, said the mystery is one which was hidden in ages past but now has been revealed to His saints, and it is *"Christ in you, the hope of glory."* He has now revealed that which was a mystery! And whatever is revealed ceases to be mysterious. In the Old Testament, God said, *"My thoughts are not your thoughts, neither are your ways my ways. For as the heavens are higher than the earth, so are my ways higher than your ways, and my thoughts than your thoughts"* (Isaiah 55:8-9). That was for the Old Testament people who did not have the eternal life of Almighty God abiding in their spirits. His ways were high above theirs as the heavens are above the earth, but now that we have become partakers of His divine nature, we have been raised up and made to sit together with Christ in heavenly places (Ephesians 2:6). That is where we live now! Glory to God!

Some people just go into the Old Testament to dig out those things that God told those folks, interpret them out of context and then try to apply them to New Testament folks. This is wrong! You have to understand that they are different from us. They were operating under a different covenant. Jesus said, *"This is my blood of the new covenant which is shed for many."* (Mark 14:24). The Bible says in Hebrew 8:13 that He has made a new covenant, thereby making the first one old; and that which decays and waxes old is ready to vanish away. In the New Testament, we have a new relationship with God, in which He has brought us to His level, so that we may know His will and understand His ways. For this reason, it is not proper for a Christian to behave lost and confused because he thinks he does not know God's will. Why not search His Word? His Word will reveal Him and His will to you.

God gives you the right to choose. You can decide what you want. You may say, "What if I choose something God does not like?" Never be afraid of that. You are a child of God, and God's will is revealed in you and to you. You are the expression of the will of God. When people see you laugh, they can tell that God laughs. People cannot see God with their optical eyes, but they see God when they see you because you are His expression! When Jesus came, He was the revelation of Almighty God. The people did not know who God was, so He told them anyone who had seen Him had seen the Father (John 14:9). *"Just watch me, listen to me, and you'll be able to tell who God is."* That's how we all should be talking because that is who we are, the expression of God.

Do not think someone is trying to dress you in borrowed robes. It is just the truth. In Acts 22:14, we find Saul of Tarsus giving his testimony. He talks of his experience on the road to Damascus: how he was blinded by a blazing light from heaven and afterwards, Jesus sent a man by the name of Ananias to him. Ananias laid hands on him and said, "Brother Saul, receive you your sight!", and he did. Then, Ananias went on to give him the message from God:

> "And he said, The God of our fathers hath chosen thee, that thou shouldest know his will, and see that Just One, and shouldest hear the voice of his mouth. For thou shalt be his witness unto all men of what thou hast seen and heard." Acts 22:14-15

Did you see that? It says, "That he should know His will." Now, you might say that was for Paul alone, but that is just what religious people would say. Yes, Paul was chosen to know God's will, and it was wonderful, but you must realize that this was not for Paul alone. It is for you too! You also have been chosen to know God's will. Take a look at Luke 4:18. Jesus was in the synagogue on a certain day and He was given the scroll to take the first reading, like it is done in some churches today. The synagogue attendant would have said, "Jesus, son of Joseph, come forward." They would not have called Him Christ because they did not know who He was.

When He stepped forward, the scroll was handed over to Him and He was told to take the first reading from the book of the Prophet Isaiah. He turned to the sixty-first chapter, and He did not read like anyone else would have read. He did not say, "Isaiah said the Spirit of the Lord was upon him (Isaiah), for the Lord hath anointed him." The other folks would have read it like that, after which they would have blessed the Name of the Lord and of His holy prophet Isaiah and gone back to their seat. When Jesus started reading, He said, *"The Spirit of the Lord is upon Me"*, referring to Himself and not Isaiah. And when He was through reading, He said, *"Today is this scripture fulfilled in your ears."*

Jesus said the Spirit of the Lord was upon Him. Why? The Bible says that heaven and earth shall pass away but the Word of God shall never pass away (Matthew 5:18). In Jesus' day, Isaiah had passed on to glory, but the Word of the Lord continued on earth, and it is still the same today. Whoever will, let him step into the Word and say, "The Spirit of the Lord is upon me", and the Holy Ghost will surely rest upon you. As a daughter, Holy Spirit rests on you!

Don't you dare think that Jesus acted the way He did because He knew Isaiah had prophesied concerning Him. If you will stand on God's Word as the disciples did, you will get the kind of results they got. Paul, writing to the churches, said the things that happened to the Old Testament folks were written down for us as examples, but the truths of the New Testament are written for us to believe and act upon today. Paul could boldly say, *"The God of our fathers has chosen me to know his will."*, but Paul has passed on to glory. Now, whosoever will, let him step into what Acts 22:14 says and declare that the God of our fathers has chosen him to know His will. That is Christianity.

God is no respecter of persons. He desired this for Paul, He desires it for you , His daughter, too. This does not infer that you are now called into one of the fivefold ministries like Paul was, but it means that you have been

94

chosen to know God's will. If you believe this, then confess it with your mouth. Say this: 'I know God's will. I am not confused. I have been chosen to know His will. Hallelujah!'

You might say, "Many are called but few are chosen." Yes, that is true, but understand it's meaning. When Jesus died on the cross, He died for everybody: Muslims, Buddhists, pagans, everyone. He died for the whole world and said, "Come unto me, all ye that labor and are heavy laden, and I will give you rest" (Matthew 11:28). The call was to everybody, but only those who answer the call and come to Jesus, i.e., become born again, are the chosen ones. How do you get chosen? When you receive the gospel of Jesus Christ and eternal life is imparted to your human spirit, you become God's choice, His chosen one. Daughter, you can therefore know His will and choose right. So, everybody has been called, but when you answer the call, you become chosen.

## YOU CAN HEAR IS VOICE

Ananias also told Paul that God had chosen him to see the Just One and to hear the voice of His mouth. That means to have a revelation of the Just On, Jesus Christ. Therefore, as His daughter, you also can boldly say, "I have been chosen to have a revelation of that Just One and to hear His voice. The whole world may hear other voices, but I can hear the voice of God, my Father." Daughter, you have been chosen to hear the voice of God. Jesus said in John 10:1-5 that He is the good Shepherd, and we are the sheep. He said when the shepherd puts forth his own sheep, He goes before

95

them, and the sheep follow Him because they know his voice. The sheep would not follow a stranger because they do not know (recognize or adhere to) the voice of strangers. Jesus used this to explain our response to His voice. For this reason, you can say confidently that you know and follow His voice.

My oldest son, his "Daddy", and I met Ron's father at the courthouse for a child support hearing. His father tried calling him to him by saying, 'Hey man, come give daddy a hug. He did not move. Then, his Daddy called to him shortly thereafter and my son ran to him. You see, he knew the voice of the one who provided for him, protected him, guided him, was there when he was sick and hospitalized, and loved him unconditionally. He recognized his voice and adhered to the command. Daughter, you too can hear the voice of your Heavenly Father and adhere to His commands.

Jesus also said that if you belong to His Father, you will hear His words and you will come to Him. For instance, you have been reading this book, and the reason you can go on reading and believing is because your spirit bears witness that this is your Father's Word. As a Christian, as His Daughter, you cannot be deceived for too long because the truth is revealed in your heart. You can only be deceived for as long as you stay outside the real teaching of God's Word and the teaching of the Spirit of God. So be assured that you can know His voice and you can choose right.

Let's revisit that question that many people ask: "What if I choose something God does not like? What if what I want is not what He wants for me?" Know this: you are a child of God, a daughter of the King of Kings. Never be afraid of that. You will know when your desire is wrong and then you can self-correct because you only experience true joy doing what He wants. Then again, you may ask, "How do I know what my Father wants?" Well, that is one of the things you have been learning in this text. Daughter, you have been chosen to know the Father's will. You have been chosen to hear and know His voice. When you were born again, The Father imparted His life into your human spirit and brought you to His realm of living (2 Peter 1:4).

You have the Spirit of God Who reveals to you the mind of The Father, so you can choose right. Do not let anybody cheat you out of God's best by telling you that you cannot choose right for yourself! You know His will and you can choose right. God has given you a right to choose. Decide what you want. Remember, Jesus asked Bartimaeus, "What do you want Me to do for you?" (Mark 10:51). Perhaps, right now you really have a need. Well then, have you told your Father what you want Him to do for you? Or are you afraid to ask? God is your heavenly Father, and He would not give you a serpent for a fish. Even if you had asked for a serpent, God would not just hand it to you. He would ask, "Daughter, what do you want a serpent for; that is dangerous for you. "

97

If you are asking wrongly, He also knows how to deal with you. He would say, "Come on daughter, that is not the right thing." He will show you the right thing. He is always out for your good. He is not out there watching and waiting for you to miss it. He is not wielding a stick over you and warning: "I have given you My will and you had better stick to it. If you do not follow My will, I will surely get you!" He does not talk like that. God is not a dictator. He is a good God. He is a loving Father.

## The Right to Live

Do you know that God has given you the right to live? Or are you one of those who say, "We are just in this world, subject to circumstances; anything can happen; nobody knows tomorrow?" When someone dies and is buried, everyone returns home wondering, Who is next? and saying, "Such is life. The Lord giveth and the Lord taketh away, blessed be the Name of the Lord forever!" They say the Lord took him, but did He, really? No! God is not a hawk! You turn on the television set and an obituary announcement comes on: "With gratitude to God, we regret to announce..." That is an oxymoron if ever there was one! They are so happy and grateful to God, and at the same time, they are so sad and full of regret for what He has done. They regretfully announce what they are grateful He did, taking their beloved one away from them. It makes no sense at all!

There is this story of a man who was very angry with God because he thought God was wicked. So, he made up his mind never to have anything to do with Him. I have heard of something like this happening all too often. When he was about 40 years old, a preacher

98

asked him why. He answered and said, "God took my mother when I was a little boy. I needed someone to take care of me, yet God took my mother away from me. I know it was Him who did it because I heard the priest say the Lord took her." When this man heard the gospel, that God is love and He never takes away from you, He only gives and does things for your good, he wept like a baby and repented.

God does not take anybody away by death. He gives you the right to live. In First Corinthians 15:26, the Bible says, "The last enemy that shall be destroyed is death." Death is an enemy. I t has already been defeated but it is going to be destroyed at the end. If God calls it an enemy, then it means that it is not God who takes people away by death. He does not require the service of death when He wants to take any one away. There are only three occasions recorded in the Bible where God took anybody away, and none was through death. Whenever anybody died, it was not said that God took him. If that person was in God's camp, he went to meet God but that did not mean it was God Who took him away. Someone else took him out, but God brought him in.

The first person we find in the Bible taken by God was Enoch.

*"And Enoch lived sixty and five years, and begat Methuselah: And Enoch walked with God after he begat Methuselah three hundred years, and begat sons and daughters: And all the*

*days of Enoch were three hundred sixty and five years: And Enoch walked with God: and he was not; for God took him."*
Genesis 5:21-24

Enoch was fellowshipping with the Lord, then he was not found anymore. The scriptures say, God took him. The Bible says he had the testimony that he pleased God, and God told him that he (Enoch) would not die, rather, that He (God) would take him. Whenever God takes somebody away, He takes him alive. **God does not use the weapon of the enemy to do anything for His children.** You may express surprise, but this is the truth. God took Enoch away alive because that is the way He does it. He takes them alive. He does not act like a hawk, meaning He would not just whisk you away suddenly on your way home. He gives you 'inside information' (intuitive knowledge) concerning when you are going.

He told Enoch, who walked outside knowing he was going because he had a testimony before his translation, that he pleased God. Hebrew 11:5: "By faith Enoch was translated that he should not see death; and was not found, because God had translated him: for before his translation he had this testimony, that he pleased God." And next comes Elijah in Second Kings 2:1-11. Elijah knew intuitively that he was going, and he told Elisha. Elisha then said, "Before you go, let a double portion of your spirit rest on me." And when they got across the Jordan, where Elijah was to be taken away, he said to Elisha, "If you see me while I am taken away, you will get what you asked for." And while they were still standing there, God sent a chariot of fire and whisked Elijah away, and Elisha saw him go! Elijah went to heaven, and it was not through death!

Both of these accounts have something in common. The two men involved knew they were going to be translated before it happened. Enoch had a testimony that he pleased God and Elijah knew he was going. God did not catch them unawares.

The third person taken away like that was Jesus. When He died, He went to hell. It was not God that took Him there. At that time, anyone who died as a sinner went to "hades" while those who died as righteous men were taken to "Abraham's bosom." Jesus was made to be sin for us, though He knew no sin (2 Corinthians 5:21) and so had to be taken to "hades" like sinners were. And it was not the angels of God who took him there, for we understand from Jude 9 that two groups are involved with what happens to the spirits of men when they die. The devil and his cohorts take their captives to hell while the angels of God come for the spirits of the saints and take them to paradise. This was before the resurrection of Jesus. Now, saints are taken to the presence of God.

When Jesus died with the sins of the whole world He was taken to hell, but He dealt with that old devil there and God raised Him from the dead on the third day. The Bible records that after His resurrection, He spent forty days with His disciples. Then one day, while talking to His disciples, He was ready to go, and God took Him away alive! The people around all saw Him as He was taken away. He gradually ascended alive until a cloud received Him out of their sight. He did not vanish, He ascended alive! (Acts 1:9).

You may ask, "What if I am old?". Look into your Bible in Genesis 5 and you will notice that most of the people lived for many years. Some lived up to 500 years. Methuselah lived for nine hundred sixty-nine years. There were others like Jared who lived for nine hundred fifty-two years, but then, they lived in sin, and God, seeing the transgressions of man, said in Genesis 6:3: "My Spirit shall not always strive with man, for that he also is flesh: yet his days shall be an hundred and twenty years." God reduced man's lifespan to one hundred twenty years, but in Psalm 90 (which was written by Moses), you will notice something different. One day, Moses was watching the children of Israel as they walked by. He shook his head and said, "The days of our years are three score years and ten (seventy): and if by reason of strength they be four score years (eighty), yet is their strength labor and sorrow; for it is soon cut off, and we fly away" (Psalm 90:10).

People have picked that up and said this is God talking through Moses; therefore, man's days are seventy to eighty years. So, when a man is above eighty years of age, they feel, "Hey, What are you still doing around?". But that wasn't God talking. It was Moses who said it, yet he lived for 120 years (Deuteronomy 34:7). Even as at the time he said that, he was already past eighty years. So, God did not hand that down.

Now, let's look at this from another angle. Let's suppose that God really did say so at that time. Jesus said in John 11:25-26, "I am the resurrection, and the life: he that believeth in Me, though he were dead, yet shall he live: And whosoever liveth and believeth in Me shall never die." Do you think He was talking about spiritual death? No! He said they shall never die. He was talking to people who were already dead spiritually. He was not talking about spiritual death, but physical death. You may be thinking, Stop right there. You have gone too far now, but I tell you, the generation of the Church of Jesus Christ that will believe this, preach it, and act on it is the generation that will see the rapture of the Church. Now, if this is something you may be struggling with, let me show you a few reasons in the Bible why you should believe it.

II Timothy 1:10 says, Jesus has abolished death, and brought life and immortality to light through the gospel. Believe me, it would rejuvenate anybody. Jesus gives you the right to live. The unconverted man may die of cancer just because he has been told by the doctor that he has cancer and has only three months to live. So, he starts to set his house in order because he believes he has cancer and has no hope. He thinks he is finished for life. He does not have the right to choose, so he just accepts whatever is handed to him. He could lose his life and all because he does not have the right to choose. For the Christian, however, it is a very different story altogether. You can decide you are not dying through cancer or asthma. You do not have to accept the verdict of the doctor as being final for your life. You have a right to choose. I remember an asthmatic woman who was caught off guard. She was on her way to a party, and she took her inhaler with her. Unknown to her, it was the empty cylinder she took. Then she had an attack. She brought out the inhaler but to her surprise, it was empty! There was no solution! She became unconscious and died on the way to the hospital. Now, if this happens to someone who is born again, s/he ought to say, "I have been born again. I have the right to live. I am not supposed to have asthma and I am not dying. I choose to live, in the Name of Jesus." You see, you have the right to choose to live and you ought to know it, stand on it, and then say, "Death, you have been defeated. You get out of my way in the Name of Jesus Christ. I am living to give glory to God in the land of the living." And that is what is going to happen. Praise God!

You may feel your situation is the worst that could ever happen to any man. You may even think that it would be better to die than to live. Thank God, He did not only give us the right to live but the right to live with dignity. When you came to Jesus, He gave you the right to live with dignity. You are no longer a nobody. You have become somebody special. Your words have power; they matter. Do you know what it was for blind Bartimaeus to call on Jesus Christ? The Bible says that when Jesus got to where he was, He stopped. This is the God of the universe stopping because a man called. That should show you that your call is important to God. You are so important to God that when you call on Him, He will stop everything else and give you His attention. Have you ever thought about that? That is how good He is and how important you are to Him.

A lot of us have never taken advantage of these things. We just stayed there suffering for months. Sometimes, you do not even know why things are happening the way they are. You just realize things are changing from what they were, and you do not know why. It is worse when you do not even know you have the right to change things. So, you stay there complaining: 'Our lives have been changing, it has been full of bitterness, we have been praying but...?' Wrong confessions are often punctuated with a "but." You, however, have a right to choose. What have you chosen? Have you even made a choice? Do not procrastinate. Choose right now! Take a piece of paper and a pen in your hand, make a definite choice and write it down. Say, "Father, I have made a choice. This is it." Now, write your choice!

### The Right to Ask for What's Yours

In Numbers 26:33, We Learn of Zelophehad's Daughters - Five sisters—Mahlah, Noah, Hoglah, Milcah, and, Tirzah, were his only children. Zelophehad was of the tribe of Manasseh, but he died in the wilderness. During that time, it was customary for fathers to leave the inheritance to sons, more specifically, the first-born son received the greater portion of the inheritance.

Several things about what the Bible tells us about these young women's lives resonates with me. The first thing is that just like these women, my dad did not have any biological sons, which means that if we were living in the era that these young women were living in, as the first-born daughter, I would be the rightful heir to his estate (never mind the fact that my daddy did not really have an estate).

The second thing that struck me was that I imagine Zelophehad taught Mahlah, Noah, Hoglah, Milcah, and Tirzah to stand up for themselves, the same way my Dad taught me. These young women recognized that they were about to be abandoned and uncared for unless they did something. So, they did just that.

You see, like other societies of that era, Israelite society was patriarchal in structure. This meant that land would pass from father to son with the provision that sons would support their widowed mothers and unmarried sisters. Since Zelophehad had no sons, the law at that time dictated that his inheritance would pass to his brothers. If no brothers, then it would be passed to his uncles.

These young women went to Moses to ask for their inheritance. Moses in turn went before the LORD and the LORD agreed that they should receive the inheritance. Daughter, you have the right to go before your Heavenly Father and ask for what is yours. The bible says you have not because you ask not. (James 4:2) There are Kingdom blessings that your Heavenly Father wants to give you. Just ask!

### The Right to Rule

Jesus has given us the right to rule.

> "And from Jesus Christ, who is the faithful witness, and the first begotten of the dead, and the prince of the kings of the earth. Unto Him that loved us and washed us from our sins in His own blood, And hath made us kings and priests unto God and his Father; to him be glory and dominion for ever and ever. Amen."

Kings rule. The Word says God has made us kings and priests, not that He *is going to make us*. He has *already* made us; He is not trying to. And if He says He has made us so, then it applies to us **now** and it remains that way. Jesus has made you a king. You are a king; it does not matter what you look like physically, you are still a king anyhow. If you are asked: "Where is your crown?" Say, "I will show you when I talk." What do I mean? You do not know kings only by their crowns, for there are many impostors.

You know kings by what happens when they talk. Let me give you an example. Let's suppose you go to an office, and you meet a small-statured man, dressed in an ordinary suit. Initially, you do not know who he is and, really, you do not care to know because he does not look like the boss. So, you greet him with less regard than you would the boss. Then in comes another gentleman, this time much bigger in stature and well-dressed and you think he is a very important person there. Although, he is not the Chief Executive, you greet him, "Good morning, sir" in a very smart and respectful manner. Then he asks you to sit and wait for the boss to see you. Now, imagine that while you are sitting there wondering who the CEO is, the small-statured man suddenly emerges from a door, snaps his fingers at the big gentleman and says, "Hey you, come in here." Then, you know who the boss really is.

After seeing the quickness with which the big gentleman responds, it immediately dawns on you who really is boss. The next time you see that small man, you will greet him with all due respect because you now know he is. This tells you that it is not in the size or material possession, but it is in what happens when you talk.

> "Where the word of a king is, there is power: and who may say unto him, what doest thou?" Ecclesiastes 8:4

You are a king, therefore, power is released when you talk. That means you must be careful to say the right things. That is why Jesus in Mark 11:23 said, *"For verily, I say unto you, that whosoever shall say unto this mountain, be thou removed, and be thou cast into the sea; and shall not doubt in his heart, but shall believe that those things which he saith shall come to pass; he shall have whatsoever he saith."* He did not say, "Whosoever says about the mountain." He said, 'Whosoever says **unto** the mountain.' It is time to rule as a king. It is time to reign in life over circumstances, sickness, lack, and poverty, as God purposed for us.

## *Exercise your Right*

*"Much more they which receive abundance of grace and of the gift of righteousness shall reign in life by one, Jesus Christ."* Romans 5:17

We have the right to choose! We have the right to live! We have the right to rule! God's Word is in support of it! You have the right to take charge and have dominion. Talk to your body; tell your body what you want. If one of your legs is shorter than the other, tell it to grow out! You ask, "Is that possible?" Yes! Tell it to grow and it will. Don't say, "I can only see five feet ahead of me." If you want to see one hundred feet ahead of you, speak to your eyes and say, "Eyes, from today, start seeing one hundred feet ahead, in the Name of Jesus Christ!" This is the way to exercise your right to choose, your right to live, and your right to rule.

Your body is not the real you. You are a spirit; you have a soul, and you live in your body (1 Thessalonians 5:23). You are the custodian of your body. You can talk to your finances; you can talk to your world. God spoke to the world (that which He had previously created) when it was in chaos. The Bible records that the whole earth was a chaotic mass **and then God said**, "Let there be light" and light came into being (Genesis 1:3). And then He put the world into order. You have your own world. Your world is your sphere of contact, your sphere of influence. What is going on in your world? What do you do when you get into someone's home and you find everyone afflicted with sickness, saying, "We do not know what is happening; everybody is falling sick. Yesterday, it was John, today it is Peter. The other day it was their father. We do not know who will be next, but we have been praying and hoping God's will will be done." They feel that talking like this makes them appear humble, but that is not humility, it is ignorance gone on rampage.

If you hear anybody talk like that, tell the person to quit talking that way. Do not sympathize with the person. If you get somewhere and they are saying things like, "Oh, there is an epidemic everywhere; it is attacking everybody!", say, "No! I am not one of them. It is not attacking everybody; at least you can count me out!"

What does the Word of God say? It says, "A thousand shall fall at thy side and ten thousand at thy right hand; but it shall not come nigh thee" (Psalm 91:7). Beloved, you have the right to choose, the right to live and the right to rule. Exercise your rights...now!

# Chapter IX

# Privileges As a Daughter of God

As a child of God (one of the redeemed who has accepted Christ as our savior and repented of our former sinful ways), we have many rights, gifts, and privileges. They are numerous, far more than I can write about in one post. So, for now, I will share with you a portion of the inheritance we have as God's children.

## Intimacy in Relationship

Christ (the Son), God (the Father), and the Holy Spirit are three distinct persons in one. So, when God sent His Son, Jesus, He was, in essence, sending Himself. It is very hard to wrap our minds around this because there is no one like Him. He exists outside of space and time, yet, we can have an intimate relationship with Him.

He paid our sin debt so that He could spend eternity with us.  He wants a relationship with us!

The Old Testament recounts how the Jewish people had to atone for their sins through regular sacrifices, and that they could not enter the temple where God's spirit dwelled.  But because of Jesus's sacrifice on the cross, we have the incredible opportunity to commune with God.  When we believe in the saving work of Jesus, His righteousness is applied to us, so that we can have an intimate relationship with the Father.  His very spirit dwells within us!

For we do not have a high priest who is unable to sympathize with our weaknesses, but one who in every respect has been tempted as we are, yet without sin.  Let us then with confidence draw near to the throne of grace, that we may receive mercy and find grace to help in time of need.  Hebrews 4:15-16

## *Abundant Life Here on Earth*

We have access to living an abundant life, which is rooted in righteousness.  Jesus said, "The thief comes only to steal and kill and destroy. I came that they may have life and have it abundantly."- John 10:10

When we are saved, we receive the Holy Spirit to help us in our sanctification process. He teaches us to live a more righteous life, to conduct ourselves to be more like our Savior.  As we grow in our relationship with the Lord and put into practice what we learn from His Word, we begin to experience an abundant and fulfilling life.

For through the Spirit we eagerly await by faith the righteousness for which we hope. For in Christ Jesus neither circumcision nor uncircumcision has any value. The only thing that counts is faith expressing itself through love. Galatians 5:5-6

Living an abundant life includes learning to forgive others, and learning to walk in the fruits of His spirit:

For if you forgive other people when they sin against you, your heavenly Father will also forgive you. – Matthew 6:14

But the fruit of the Spirit is love, joy, peace, patience, kindness, goodness, faithfulness, gentleness, and self-control. Against such things there is no law. Those who belong to Christ Jesus have crucified the flesh with its passions and desires. Since we live by the Spirit, let us keep in step with the Spirit. Galatians 5:22-25

## Loving Discipline

Good parents discipline their children in a loving and teaching way, and sometimes that means allowing their children to learn from a lesser pain or mistake to prevent far greater pain in the future. We have the privilege of being disciplined by our loving Heavenly Father who cares for us deeply and wants what is best for us.

They disciplined us for a little while as they thought best; but God disciplines us for our good, in order that we may share in his holiness. No discipline seems pleasant at the time, but painful. Later on, however, it produces a harvest of righteousness and peace for those who have been trained by it. – Hebrews 12:10-11

This discipline changes us and prepares us for the work God has called us to do.

All Scripture is God-breathed and is useful for teaching, rebuking, correcting, and training in righteousness, so that the servant of God may be thoroughly equipped for every good work. II Timothy 3:16-17

## Authority & Power

Just as a prince or princess of an earthly kingdom would carry the authority from the king or queen, we carry the authority of our Father over evil, and we have been given power through His Holy Spirit to complete the assignment He has commissioned us with; telling others the good news about Jesus.

And Jesus came and said to them, "All authority in heaven and on earth has been given to me. Go therefore and make disciples of all nations, baptizing them in the name of the Father and of the Son and of the Holy Spirit." - Matthew 28:18-19

And He called the twelve together and gave them power and authority over all the demons and to heal disease...– Luke 9:1

Truly, truly I say to you, he who believes in Me, the works that I do, he will do also; and greater works than these he will do; because I go to the Father. – John 14:12

## Security & Assurance Through Everlasting Life

Every human being, except Jesus Christ, has sinned. The penalty for sin is death and eternal separation from our Heavenly Father, but when we accept Jesus's substitutionary sacrifice as payment for our sin, we are pardoned. As children of God, we have the single greatest gift imaginable, the security of eternal life with Him. We also have the assurance that once we give our life to Him and live for Him, we are His forever.

Jesus said, "My sheep hear my voice, and I know them, and they follow me. I give them eternal life, and they will never perish, and no one will snatch them out of my hand." – John 10:27-28

While this list has by no means been exhaustive, it includes some of the main highlights of our inheritance as children of God. I would like to encourage you to meditate on these things and ask God to speak to your heart and give you an even greater understanding of who He is and who you are in Christ.

# Chapter X

# Significance of Sonship

As previously stated, sonship in the kingdom of God is a generic term used for both male and female, and it refers to those that the Spirit of God has adopted. One of our greatest needs is to know that we are individually and personally a child of God. Not only is this one of believers' greatest assurances, but the quality of the experience of being a son or daughter of God marks the relationship as the greatest of all privileges.

To be able to call upon God as our Heavenly Father because we are "in Christ" is the ultimate reason and meaning of our faith and the basis for meaningful Christian living (cf Galatians 3:26-29). In Romans 8:12-18, the apostle Paul specifies for us the Significance of Sonship. Paul asserts that being a child of God means:

I.     Obligation (vv 12-13)
II.    Assurance (vv 14-16)
III.   Privilege (vs 17)

The word "adoption" occurs five times in the New Testament (Greek huiothesia). Paul is the only New Testament writer to use the term, and with him it is a metaphor derived from Hellenistic usage and Roman law. In Galatians 4:1-3 Paul accurately interprets the Roman law of sonship. In verse four he says that God sent His Son to be born into the human condition under law, and in verse five the purpose of God's action was "to redeem them that were under the law, that we might receive the adoption of sons."

We were not merely children who needed to mature; we had become enslaved to sin and needed to be redeemed--bought out of bondage--that we might enter the new family which Christ created by His death and resurrection. Adoption means both the redemption and the new relation of trust and love, for "*because you are sons, God has sent forth the Spirit of His Son into your hearts, crying, Abba, Father*" (vs 6). The adoption freed us from slavery to sonship and inheritance (vs 7).

Ephesians 4:6 states there is one "God and Father of all, who is above all, and through all, and in you all." The third phrase, "in you all," speaks of God's indwelling and suggests a personal and intimate relationship. To be a child of God means that our Heavenly Father dwells "in" His people by His Spirit. The indwelling presence of the living God demands a different, transformed life. To be a child of the King is to be blessed and beloved of God; yet there is no privilege without responsibility.

I.      Paul strongly asserts that being God's child involves obligation (vv 12-13). To be called a child of God carries with it a necessary consequence - "we are debtors." We owe an obligation, a duty, but our duty is not owed "to the flesh," so that we should live according to its demands but is rather owed to the Spirit of God. As brothers and sisters in Christ, we are obligated to our Father who bought us with the price of Christ's blood, to live our lives according to the direction and control of His Spirit.
In First Corinthians 6:19-20, Paul declares: "Do you not know that your body is a temple of the Holy Spirit within you, which you have from God? You are not your own; you were bought with a price. So, glorify God in your body." This means that as a child of God we are not to profane His Holy Spirit through impure, immoral, or unhealthy living; but rather, we are to live God-honoring lives - lives that would allow the Holy Spirit to dwell in a clean, fit vessel, a holy sanctuary (tabernacle).

Paul states the case for holy living in Romans 12:1 when he says you are to "present your bodies a living sacrifice, holy, acceptable to God, which is your reasonable service." The obligation of sonship is so great that it may even demand a martyr's death for the cause of Christ. Yet He calls each one of us to a life of service and commitment. Some may be willing to give their lifeblood on the altar of sacrifice, to literally die for Him, but how many are willing to live for Him?

The duty of being a child of God is not to glorify self but to glorify Him who called us to be His own. Self-glorification makes impossible the glorification of God. Christ himself, the Son of God who shows us the true example of sonship, says we are to be "the salt of the earth"...and "light of the world." "Let your light so shine before men, that they may see your good works and glorify your Father which is in heaven" (Matthew 5:13-16).

We often fail to fulfill our duty to honor God because of our own petty and selfish concerns. Remember that even a penny, when held too close to the eye, will blot out the brilliance of the sun. Likewise, we as the children of God, often eclipse God's glory and greatness because of our pride and self-seeking ambitions. The Bible reminds us that spiritual pride is the root of all evil (cf Genesis 3:5; 1 Timothy 3:6; 1 John 2:15-17).

II.  Paul further states that being a child of God involves assurance (vv 14-16). The hope of life is based upon the assurance that we "are the sons of God." The evidence of being a child of God is an awareness of the presence, leadership, and fellowship of the Holy Spirit. The peace of His presence provides a confidence and a hope that is beyond human understanding. Our assurance as God's child is that if God be for us, who can be against us? We have confidence because we "did not receive a spirit of slavery to fall back into fear" (vs 15). Second Timothy 1:7 declares that God has not given us the spirit of fear; but of power, and of love, and of a sound mind (self-control, discipline).

Each relationship of life has its appropriate emotion: in slavery it is fear; in the family of God, it is confidence and grateful joy. As a child of God, we have been delivered from the bondage of fear and death. Our hope is that we are even more than conquerors through Him who loves us (Romans 8:37). When we cry, "Abba, Father" we are expressing a quiet confidence in approaching God as children to a father. Having been adopted into the family of God by His grace, we have access to Him in an intimate kind of fellowship (cf Matthew 6:32). This glorious freedom and liberty of being God's child is possible because our relationship to God the Father is one of love. "And there is no fear in love; but perfect love casts out fear" (1 John 4:18).

The final basis for the assurance of being God's child is the testimony of God's Spirit "bearing witness with our Spirit that we are children of God" (vs 16). If we are truly a child of God, self-confirmation will come through the joint witness of the Holy Spirit with our spirits. But not only does sonship signify obligation and assurance, but...

III. Paul declares that being a child of God involves privilege (vv 17-18). As a result of being "children of God," we discover that we are "heirs" as well. If even the child of an earthly household can look forward confidently to receive his/her due share of all the resources that the father/parent possesses, how much greater is the inheritance of the child of God. As heirs of God, we are privileged not only to enjoy eternal life in Heaven, but to enjoy the blessings of His abundant life even now.

The tragedy of our lives is that God has placed untold millions in our name in the bank account of life, and we are content to write checks for petty cash. Corrie ten Boom, Dutch evangelist who survived the Holocaust, said, "*Jesus Christ opens wide the doors of the treasure-house of God's promises and bids us go in and take with boldness the riches that are ours [as God's children].*" The privilege of being God's child goes beyond being merely "heirs" but we are "joint heirs with Christ," meaning that we partake of all that the resurrection of Christ implies. We will be glorified with Christ, provided we suffer with Him (cf Philippians 1:29 and Philippians 3:10).

The benefits and privileges of being a child of God are available to everyone willing to satisfy the necessary conditions. The cost of sonship and discipleship is high...it costs us our very lives, but the new life in Christ given in exchange for our old lives is so far greater, it is not to be compared. If we are willing to receive the life God offers us in Christ, then through repentance and faith we can become children of God.

> "But as many as received Him, to them gave the power to become children of God, even to them that believe on His name" (John 1:12).

Have you experienced the assurance and joy of being a part of the family of God? If you are certain of your relationship to God as Father, are you fulfilling your obligation as an obedient child? You can know the privileges and blessings of belonging to the Father if you will totally commit your life to the will of God.
Jesus says, "If you have seen me, you have seen the Father." He further declares, "I am the Way, the Truth, and the Life; no one comes to the Father, but by me" (John 14:6).

Will you follow Christ into the wonderful experience of being His brother or sister? You will be eternally grateful to God for taking this most important of all steps and making this wisest of all decisions. Jesus never offers a smooth path or an easy journey, but He does promise to be with us. God gives us the ultimate victory over suffering, sin, and death so that the glory that will be ours is beyond comparing what we face in this world (vs 18). Bad things can and do happen to good people. Bad things happened to Jesus, the Son of God, but the Lord promises ultimate victory for all those in Christ, the children of God who trust a loving Heavenly Father.

# Bibliography

# Bibliography

(n.d.). Retrieved from www.merriam-webster.com: https://www.merriam-webster.com/dictionary/orphan

*11 Contrasting Traits between an Orphan Spirit and a Spirit of Sonship.* (2017, March 16). Retrieved from Joseph Mattera: https://josephmattera.org/eleven-contrasting-traits-between-an-orphan-spirit-and-a-spirit-of-sonship/

*Adoption in Chrst: A Story of Unimaginably Good News.* (n.d.). Retrieved from Union: https://www.uniontheology.org/resources/doctrine/adoption-in-christ-a-story-of-unimaginably-good-news

Angela Joyce. (2022, February 25). *The Leading Causes of Orphans Today.* Retrieved from Life: https://www.lifeusa.org/post/the-leading-causes-of-orphans-today

Banso, P. (2020, February 28). *Dealing with the Gehazi in You.* Retrieved from Cedar Ministry: https://cedarministry.org/dealing-with-the-gehazi-in-you/

*Behind the Chair Ministries.* (n.d.). Retrieved from Behind the Chair Ministries: https://behindthechairministries.com/articles/orphan-spirit

Bradley, D. (2023, August 23). *Aesthetic Procedures Are at an All-Time High, but People Are Getting Left Behind.* Retrieved from Think Global Health: https://www.thinkglobalhealth.org/article/aesthetic-procedures-are-all-time-high-people-are-

getting-left-
behind#:~:text=According%20to%20a%20recent
%20global,an%20all%2Dtime%20high%20worldwid
e.

Bucher, M. (2020, August 11). *The Power and Joy of Being in the Family of God*. Retrieved from Bible Study Tools: https://www.biblestudytools.com/bible-study/topical-studies/the-power-and-joy-of-being-in-the-family-of-god.html

Calder, H. (n.d.). *4 Symptoms of the Orphan Spirit in Church Life*. Retrieved from Enliven Publishing: https://www.enlivenpublishing.com/2012/09/17/4-symptoms-of-the-orphan-spirit-in-church-life/

*Collins Dictionary*. (n.d.). Retrieved from Collins Dictionary: https://www.collinsdictionary.com/us/dictionary/english/sheepish#:~:text=If%20you%20look%20she epish%2C%20you,little%20sheepish%20when%20h e%20answered.&text=He%20grinned%20sheepishl y.

Collmorgen, S. (2020, October 29). *Our Right and Privileges as Children of God*. Retrieved from Dedicated to Christ: https://www.dedicatedtochrist.org/blog/948973/our-rights-and-privileges-as-children-of-god

Copeland, K. (2018, March 6). *Your Rights as a Child of God*. Retrieved from KCM.org: https://blog.kcm.org/rights-child-god/

*dictionary.cambridge.org*. (n.d.). Retrieved from Cambridge Dictionary: https://dictionary.cambridge.org/us/dictionary/e nglish/shout-out

*Five Benefits of Being Adopted as Children into God's Family*. (n.d.). Retrieved from West Ridge Church:

https://westridge.com/five-benefits-of-being-adopted-as-children-into-gods-family/

Hetland, L. (2020). *Healing the Orphan Spirit*. Leif Hetland.

Joyce, A. (2022, February 25). *The Leading Causes of Orphans Today*. Retrieved from Life: https://www.lifeusa.org/post/the-leading-causes-of-orphans-today

Landry, C. (2018, January 29). *Is the Orphan Spirit Operatiing in My Life*. Retrieved from Curt Landry Ministries: https://www.curtlandry.com/is-the-orphan-spirit-operating-in-my-life/

Mattera, J. (n.d.). *Shady Oaks Church*. Retrieved from https://shadyoakschurch.org/: https://shadyoakschurch.org/wp-content/uploads/2018/07/The-Difference-Between-the-Orphan-Spirit-and-a-Spirit-of-Sonship.pdf

*Merriam Webster*. (n.d.). Retrieved from https://www.merriam-webster.com: https://www.merriam-webster.com/dictionary/rejection

Moore, A. (n.d.). *Behing the Chair Ministries*. Retrieved from https://behindthechairministries.com/: https://behindthechairministries.com/articles/orphan-spirit

Oyakhilome, C. (1998). *Your Rights in Christ*. Retrieved from Christian Diet: https://christiandiet.com.ng/wp-content/uploads/2020/06/Your-Rights-In-Christ-Chris-Oyakhilome-Christiandiet.com_.ng_.pdf

Parsons, M. (n.d.). *Orphan Spirit - Sons of Issachar*. Retrieved from Freedom Apostolic Ministries: https://freedomarc.blog/tag/orphan-spirit/

*Preaching: The Holy Spirit #9 - The Spirit of Adoption*. (n.d.). Retrieved from Gainsville Presbyterian

Church: https://www.gpcweb.org/the-holy-spirit--9-the-spirit-of-adoption

Ray Deck, I. (n.d.). *Logos Bible Software*. Retrieved from https://www.logos.com/grow/7-things-the-bible-says-about-orphans/#:~:text=The%20Hebrew%20word%20for%20orphan,unwilling%20to%20care%20for%20them.

Red, M. (n.d.). *Urban Dictionary*. Retrieved from https://www.urbandictionary.com/define.php?term=Joning

Roberts, J. W. (1982). Joning: An Afro-American Verbal Form in St. Louis. *Journal of the Folklore Institute*, 19(1), 61-70.

Sharon Kaplan Roszia, A. D. (2019, July). *Seven Core Issues in Adoption and Permanency*. Retrieved from NACAC - North American Council on Adoptable Children: https://nacac.org/resource/seven-core-issues-in-adoption-and-permanency/#:~:text=Seven%20Core%20Issues%20in%20Adoption%20and%20Permanency%2C%20which%20include%20loss,of%20a%20new%20family%20system.

*The Prodigal Son*. (n.d.). Retrieved from thyword is truth.com: http://www.thywordistruth.com/sermon/prodigal.pdf

*What is an Orphan Spirit? 16+ Character Traits*. (2022, July 10). Retrieved from Adorned Heart: https://www.adornedheart.com/what-is-an-orphan-spirit-characteristics/

Wood, D. W. (2021, June 23). *Significance of Sonship: Adoption as a Child of God*. Retrieved from Linked In: https://www.linkedin.com/pulse/significance-

sonship-adoption-child-god-darrell-w-
wood#:~:text=The%20privilege%20of%20being%2
0God's,and%20Philippians%203%3A10).

Zehr, A. (2019, July 31). *5 Examples of Adoption in the Bible*. Retrieved from Life Song for Orphans:
https://lifesong.org/2019/07/example-adoption-
bible/#:~:text=God%20heard%20her%20prayer%2
C%20and,raised%20to%20be%20a%20prophet.

(Bradley, 2023)

# Author Bio

 Dr. LaTatia Whitaker-Riley - Author – Preacher – Christian Counselor and Entrepreneur - has a passion for helping women push pass fear, guilt and shame, and into their purpose. She is the CEO of La'Whit-Riley Enterprises, International, and a dynamic motivational speaker. She earned her Master of Christian Counseling, and Doctor of Theology from Word of Prayer Bible Institute, both Cum Laude. A native of Washington, DC, she is happily reunited with and married to Marcellus, her junior high school sweetheart, still living in the DMV. Dr. Whitaker-Riley is an Elder and the Women's Ministry Director at Life Redemption Church in Alexandria, VA. For more information you can find her on Instagram.com/lawhitriley.

Made in the USA
Columbia, SC
11 August 2024

39814175R00085